MOBTOWN
MASSACRE

Alexander Hanson and the Baltimore Newspaper War of 1812

Josh S. Cutler

Foreword by Dr. Edward Papenfuse

THE
Hi**st**ory
PRESS

Published by The History Press
Charleston, SC
www.historypress.com

Front cover: *The Conspiracy against Baltimore or The War Dance at Montgomery Court House*, 1812 engraving by unknown artist. *Courtesy of the Maryland Historical Society*.

First published 2019

Manufactured in the United States

ISBN 9781467142274

Library of Congress Control Number: 2018960976

For Dad

CONTENTS

CONTENTS

HANSON:
PROTEST AND RIOT OF 1812

A s anyone who has studied civic unrest and mob action knows, mobs can, and often do, take on a mind of their own, leading to unintended consequences of property destruction and death. Paul Gilje, in his seminal article on the Baltimore mob of the summer of 1812 (*Journal of Social History* 13, no. 4 (Summer 1980): 547–64), probes one of the earliest mob actions in the life of the republic and gave Baltimore the nickname of *Mobtown*, a moniker that the city has not been able to live down to the present day when attempting to deal with the aftermath of the death of Freddie Gray. In the latter instance, the city authorities acted quickly to stem the excesses of what began as a reasonable political protest on the part of high school students and mushroomed into a looting spree successfully contained without bloodshed. The circumstances in the summer of 1812 were different. Civic leadership was bewildered and uncertain how to act. The mob ruled, resulting in the death of a Revolutionary War hero and the severe beating of the newspaper editor who, undoubtedly, with his printed words and his provocative actions, precipitated the violence.

The Baltimore riots and mob action of the summer of 1812 had their origins in a written war between two Baltimore newspaper editors—Alexander Contee Hanson and Baptis Irvine—in the context of a bitter party rivalry that pitted Jeffersonian Democrat-Republicans against Washington-worshiping Federalists. In its most basic form, the Democrats favored punitive action against Great Britain for its depredations of American shipping and the impressment of American sailors on the high seas, while the Washington

Federalists opposed war and favored the first president's caution against foreign entanglements. Beginning as early as 1808 in the pages of the *Baltimore Whig* (Irvine's newspaper) and the *Baltimore Republican* (Alexander Contee Hanson's newspaper) and pursued in the courts, Hanson and Irvine battled it out in print and before juries. The courts (including a court-martial of Hanson for refusing to take up arms against the British) found in favor of Hanson. Irvine smarted and perhaps played an instrumental role in whipping up the mob to destroy the printing office of Hanson's in Baltimore and then pursue Hanson and his associates to their bloody beating when Hanson returned to reestablish the paper and his voice in the city.

Paul Gilje's article provides a succinct account of the mob's emergence and actions. It is rightfully critical of the assault on the freedom of the press and provides a useful overview of the story that Josh Cutler tells so well in the following pages. Here in an engaging narrative drawn from the literally hundreds of pages of testimony, court records and editorial comment from around the infant nation, the full story of Alexander Contee Hanson's defense of an unfettered press is told with readable fairness and a sense of the times that leave the reader fulfilled by the story but wanting to know more, eager for the next installment.

It is perhaps fair to say that Baltimore in the first two decades of the nineteenth century is an enigma that historians have yet to fully puzzle out and unravel. It was an urban miracle in the midst of a slaveholding plantation society that within a small geographical imprint expanded from 8 percent of the total population of Maryland to a nearly doubled 15 percent by 1820, including a rapidly growing free black population that posed a rising threat to the stability of the rest of the slaveholding state. In those years, the focus of the city was on its commercial expansion, both legal and extralegal. Baltimore was notorious for its advocacy of disrupting and capturing "enemy" shipping, supplying rebels in Central and South America, and in the expansion of American territory to the north and to the south. New Orleans became a trading partner of the highest order both in agricultural products (rice, sugar and cotton) and slaves. Protecting that trade from the depredations of the British and advocating expansion of territory and trade into Canada was the objective of its merchants and the war cry of the mob.

In this narrative, Josh Cutler focuses on the story of what happened in Baltimore in those summer months of 1812, raising the specter that the actions of Alexander Contee Hanson were motivated in part by a desire to advance his own political career. Whether or not that was the case, Hanson did win his election to Congress that fall, galvanizing the electorate in support of the Federalists statewide. For the next decade, the Federalists would control the general assembly and the statehouse, and Alexander Contee Hanson would become a U.S. senator from Maryland, a post he held until his death at thirty-three in 1819.

As to the leaders of the mob of the summer of 1812 and their followers, they were acquitted by juries of their peers and lived to lead another day, with perhaps the greatest irony being the career of the butcher Mumma, who probably led the assault on the jail that led to death of General Lingan and who by 1820 was no less a justice of the peace in the city. As to Baptis Irvine, he persisted in his advocacy of war and participated in the invasion of Canada as the second lieutenant of the First Baltimore Volunteers, who raised the American flag over York, Canada, and helped torch the Canadian capital, an action that the British claimed was their reason for burning public buildings in Washington, D.C., in the summer of 1814. Irvine may also have been the first imbedded reporter in a military unit, as his reports of his and his unit's exploits along the Canadian border were published in the *Baltimore Whig*. Not all of the Americans on the New York side of the border were pleased with the presence of the Baltimore Volunteers, known locally around Buffalo as the "Baltimore Greens," One local history of Buffalo, New York, recalls:

> *A call was made by the Government for volunteers, and troops of all ranks and arms, were hurried on to the Niagara frontier. Amongst the troops sent to Buffalo, was a company from Baltimore, called the "Baltimore Greens." It is said this company was composed almost entirely of men who were engaged in the great riot, in that city, a few months previous ; that they had been enlisted by the citizens of Baltimore for the double purpose of aiding the Government in the war, and to get rid of a very dangerous and troublesome body of men. This company came to Buffalo in the Summer of 1812 ; feel- ing but little the restraints of discipline, they visited the houses demanding food and drink of the inhabitants, as a right which they claimed as the defenders of the place against a foreign enemy.*

—An Authentic and Comprehensive History of Buffalo, with Some Account of Its Early Inhabitants Both Savage and Civilized, Comprising Historic Notices of the Six Nations or Iroquois Indians, including a Sketch of the Life of Sir William Johnson, and of Other Prominent White Men, Long Resident among the Senecas Arranged in Chronological Order *by William Ketchum, Buffalo, New York, 1864, p. 237*

Whether or not the formation of the "Baltimore Greens" was an attempt to get the worst of the participants in the mob safely out of town is accurate, at least one of the participants identified in the mob, George Hayes, appears on the muster roll of the First Baltimore Volunteers, the formal name of Lieutenant Baptis Irvine's militia company.

In the narrative that follows, Josh S. Cutler takes the reader on a journey that is as relevant today as it was two hundred years ago. Freedom of the press is essential to the future of our democracy. Attacking that right, both verbally and physically, can have dire consequences. Every effort should be made to counter fake news and unjust hyperbole with accurate and balanced reporting, but that does not extend to violence or bullying tactics. Both Hanson and Irvine took their written exchanges in the press to a level that incited violence and had consequences that even leaders like Butcher Mumma purported came to regret.

Seeking public discourse that is civil and well informed is not easily accomplished and requires a level of emphasis on civic education that was not present in 1812 and seems to be increasingly absent today. There are lessons to be learned from the Baltimore mob actions of the summer of 1812 that remain unlearned. Josh Cutler's narrative, apart from its entertainment value, should prove a useful and instructive resource for those who would chart a more positive course for American political behavior.

—Dr. Edward C. Papenfuse,
Maryland State Archivist, retired

ACKNOWLEDGEMENTS

I t's been a joy to peel back the layers of history and get to know Alexander Contee Hanson, one of the more admirable and irascible American characters of the nineteenth century. Few figures in the history of our nation risked more to defend the principle of the free press—both with the pen and the pistol. His story has fascinated me ever since I first discovered that the quiet little town of Hanson, Massachusetts, was named after a not-so-quiet newspaper publisher from Maryland.

I am grateful to all who have provided assistance for this project. Thanks to my team of beta readers for guidance and feedback, including Meg Chandler, and especially my mother, Suzanne Cutler, who dutifully marked up each chapter as it was completed. I also owe a special note of thanks to David A. Mittell Jr., who was most generous with his time, editing skills and positive encouragement. I'm reminded of the advice of my late father: adverbs and adjectives are tools of the weak mind; let your verbs and nouns tell the story. Thanks to Lori Sullivan for joining me in the adventure—literally and figuratively—including helping with the often-challenging task of deciphering two-hundred-year old handwritten letters. (And I thought my handwriting was bad!)

I can't say enough good things about the Maryland Historical Society. It's a fantastic resource, and it has a rich treasure of documents about the War of 1812, Baltimore and the Hanson family. I'd like to thank the staff at the Special Collections desk, including Damon Talbot, and Dan Goodrich for assistance with images. The *Maryland Historical Magazine* archives also were invaluable. The Maryland State Archives is another great resource; thanks to Kevin Swanson for assistance digging up old Maryland court dockets.

Noted Maryland historian Dr. Edward Papenfuse was kind enough offer advice and insight on many occasions and share some of his boundless knowledge of Baltimore history. Don't miss his "Tuesdays with Ed" at the Baltimore City Archives. ("Better call Saul!") Thanks also to Rob Schoeberlein at BCA for digging up old city council minutes.

The folks at the Belmont Manor Estate in Elkridge, Maryland, were gracious and generous in sharing information, including manager Catherine Allen and historian Fred Dorsey. Even if you're not a history buff, Belmont is worth a visit—and it's a great spot for a wedding.

Thank you to the Howard County Historical Society and the staff of its Archives and Research Library in Ellicott City, including Executive Director Shawn Gladden and Assistant Director Paulette Lutz. I was able to track down old issues of the *Frederick-Town Herald* with help from Kaitlyn and Olivia of Heritage Frederick (formerly Historical Society of Frederick County). For additional background on Hanson's home in Rockville, I looked to the Montgomery County Historical Society. The Baltimore History Facebook group managed by Mike Franch was another helpful resource, as were Chip Markell and the Baltimore City Historical Society. A note of thanks also to the Maryland Society of the War of 1812, the Clifton House (including Susan Brooks and John Ciekot), the Baltimore County Historical Society and to *Niles Weekly Register* index editor Bill Earle for research assistance.

On the Massachusetts end, there also are a number of folks and organizations I'd like to acknowledge. The Boston Athenæum was a great resource in my early research, as was the Massachusetts State House Library, including Silvia Mejia, Special Collections librarian. The staff at the Massachusetts Historical Society were fantastic and highly responsive. The Digital Commonwealth is another great online resource, and my Boston Public Library card opened the door to many more online resources.

Thanks to John Norton and the Hanson Historical Society for their interest in this project and for inviting me to their meeting to offer a presentation. I'm looking forward to celebrating the town's 200th anniversary in 2020 and sharing more about the town's illustrious namesake. Karen Proctor of the Pembroke Historical Society also provided valuable guidance.

I'd like to thank the staff at the *New England History Journal*, including Linda Morse, Erin Redihan and Gwen Carlill, for their assistance publishing a shorter companion article last spring. The peer review process certainly helped me sharpen my pencil.

Jon Cullen got me excited about writing again, and good pals Tom O'Brien, Jim Cantwell and Chris Shipps provided support along the way. Thanks also to Becky Coletta, Joe Pelligra and Cole Angley.

To paraphrase wiser folks than I, some projects are never truly completed, merely abandoned. I feel that way about this narrative. Every time I think I've reached the finish line, there's a new lead or historical tidbit to track down. Thank heavens for deadlines and for the good folks at The History Press. I hope readers enjoy the final product as much as I've enjoyed writing it. This may be a story about a window in time over two hundred years ago, but it offers some lessons for us even today.

PROLOGUE

We must have them out; blood cries for blood!

BALTIMORE, JULY 28, 1812—Working by torchlight and armed with hatchets, clubs and crowbars, the mob rushed into the courtyard of the Baltimore Jail just after sunset. A military drum and fife could be heard in the distance. Thirty to forty men swarmed in and brushed past the remaining guards.

The city's militia commander had already retired to bed after dismissing his troops, but most hadn't reported for duty in the first place—they viewed the prisoners inside as traitors. The soldiers who did appear were instructed not to carry ammunition and rely on their bayonets for protection, but not all obeyed that order either.

A hot-tempered shoemaker led the rioters, whose ranks were filled with a combustible mixture of shopkeepers, craftsmen, disgruntled militia and working-class immigrants—mainly Irish and German. Many had come from Fell's Point, a gritty dockside neighborhood outside Baltimore's Old Town, where the jail was located. Whether foreign or native, laborer or master craftsman, the rioters were united in their mission on this night.

"Where are those murdering scoundrels who…slaughtered our citizens in cold blood!" the shoemaker yelled as the mob charged into the jail yard. "We must have them out; blood cries for blood!"

It was no idle threat. The shoemaker had recently been the ringleader of another mob and was once convicted of beating, tarring and feathering a British shoemaker who had made "anti-American" remarks.

Baltimore City Jail by J.H. Latrobe. *Johns Hopkins University.*

Inside the yard, the mayor, sheriff and a handful of citizens stood by, hoping to prevent further violence. The mayor was sympathetic to the rioters and no fan of the imprisoned agitators he was now charged with protecting. He approached the mob's leaders to assure them that the prisoners would not be let loose on bail.

"It is not yet too late; support me, and we may prevent the horrid scene," he said.

But the mob would not be dissuaded, and the mayor was pushed aside. The shoemaker and his fellow rioters began attacking the wooden jail door with axes and hatchets, while another group of men circled around to the front steps. The jail door opened, possibly from the inside by a sympathetic jail keeper, and the mob burst into the brick building. Using sledgehammers and crowbars, they went to work on a heavy inner door protected by metal gratings, eventually forcing it open and gaining entry to the passageway leading to the cells.

Trapped inside on the bare floor, more than a dozen men contemplated their fates. This cell was usually reserved for the "rogues," but these were no ordinary criminals. Their ranks included a general who fought alongside George Washington, a famed Revolutionary War hero, and their young leader—a twenty-six-year-old newspaper editor named Alexander Hanson.

Hanson's gravitas sprang from his intellect rather than his physical stature. He was a man of slight features and diminutive build, usually well dressed and groomed. Like most young men of his era, Hanson had abandoned the powdered wigs of his grandfather's generation in favor of a more classical and natural look—clean shaven, save for a pair of long sideburns, with a head of short, unruly curls. Unruly could also apply to his personality, for his patrician upbringing belied a fierce temperament, just as his weak constitution masked an iron will.

Alexander Contee Hanson Jr. *Library of Congress.*

Hanson and his fellow prisoners heard the beating drums and knew the mob had gathered outside, yet they clung to the hope that the local militia commander would return to offer protection. At some point during the night, the fire bell began to ring, but no help was forthcoming. The whoops and hollers of the rioters grew louder, and one last door stood between the prisoners and the mob. The cell door was locked, but somehow the rioters ended up with a key.

With the mob closing in, the prisoners formulated a quick plan. They were vastly outnumbered and outgunned, but still they hoped the element of surprise might allow some of them to escape the massacre they feared was coming. Some in the group counseled a direct frontal assault with the few weapons on hand, but Hanson knew that would only take down a few men and further enrage the mob. He convinced his fellow prisoners to follow an alternate course even though it put his own life in peril. As the final heavy iron door swung open, the prisoners sprang into action.

The aftermath of the confrontation would end lives, launch careers, capture headlines and leave a bloody stain on the halls of the jail and the city of Baltimore itself. When the dust eventually settled, the episode sent shock waves across the country and ultimately helped shape the course of a war, a political party and the nation's very notion of freedom of the press.

It all began with a headline.

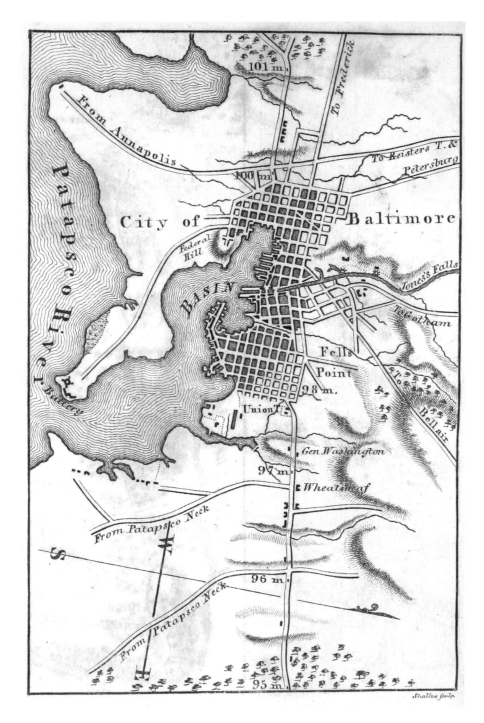

THE EDITORIAL

Thou has done a deed, whereat valor will weep.

Baltimore, June 20, 1812 (*Five weeks earlier*)—It wasn't President James Madison's declaration of war against Great Britain that drew the attention of most Baltimore readers on this warm Saturday morning in June. The new edition of the paper was most notable for an editorial published on the back of the two-page broadsheet.

The appearance of the words themselves was unremarkable. Set in small type in a roman serif font, they were sandwiched around news of daily ship arrivals in the Port of Baltimore, an update on the Maryland state legislature and a classified notice from a husband cross about his wife's spendthrift ways. Only the single-column headline, italic font, hinted at the content to come: "Thou has done a deed, whereat valor will weep."

The quotation hails from Shakespeare's tragedy *Coriolanus*, about a Roman military hero who fails in the political realm and is later assassinated. The dramatic literary reference was no accident. The *Federal Republican*, one of a half-dozen newspapers covering Baltimore after the turn of the nineteenth century, was known for its incendiary rhetoric and strident views. In an era dominated by the partisan press, the radical Federalist newspaper stood out.[1]

Now that the young nation had declared war for the first time in its history, the Saturday edition was eagerly anticipated. What would the newspaper and its fiery editor have to say about this development? The vote for war in Congress was a close one, divided along party and regional lines.

Right: President James Madison was a disciple of Thomas Jefferson's and helped found the Democratic-Republican Party. *Library of Congress*.

Below: Madison's formal declaration in June started the War of 1812 against Great Britain. *Library of Congress*.

BY THE PRESIDENT
OF THE
United States of America,
A PROCLAMATION:

WHEREAS the Congress of the United States, by virtue of the Constituted Authority vested in them, have declared by their act, bearing date the eighteenth day of the present month, that WAR exists between the United Kingdom of Great Britain and Ireland, and the dependencies thereof, and the United States of America and their territories; Now, therefore, I, JAMES MADISON, President of the United States of America, do hereby proclaim the same to all whom it may concern: and I do specially enjoin on all persons holding offices, civil or military, under the authority of the United States, that they be vigilant and zealous, in discharging the duties respectively incident thereto: And I do moreover exhort all the good people of the United States, as they love their country; as they value the precious heritage derived from the virtue and valor of their fathers; as they feel the wrongs which have forced on them the last resort of injured nations; and as they consult the best means, under the blessing of Divine Providence, of abridging its calamities; that they exert themselves in preserving order, in promoting concord, in maintaining the authority and the efficacy of the laws, and in supporting and invigorating all the measures which may be adopted by the Constituted Authorities, for obtaining a speedy, a just, and an honorable peace.

IN TESTIMONY WHEREOF I have hereunto set my hand, and caused the seal of the United States to be affixed to these presents.

(SEAL.)

DONE at the City of Washington, the nineteenth day of June, one thousand eight hundred and twelve, and of the Independence of the United States the thirty-sixth.

(Signed) JAMES MADISON,

By the President,
(Signed) JAMES MONROE, Secretary of State.

The Federalist versus Republican political divide was a microcosm of a broader conflict between Great Britain and France. Federalists saw the French leader Napoleon as the greater threat, while the Republicans identified more with France and shared its hostility to the British monarchy. In this pro-Federalist political cartoon, President Madison is depicted between Napoleon and the Devil while Great Britain looks on. *Library of Congress.*

Federalists, concentrated in New England and the Mid-Atlantic, vigorously opposed the war and argued the nation was ill-prepared for another foreign entanglement, especially against Great Britain, the world's greatest naval power.

Republicans, or Democratic-Republicans as they were also known,[2] broadly supported the war and felt the nation had little choice given British tariffs, attacks on American sailors and incitement of Native American warfare on the western frontier.

Perched in the middle ground geographically and politically, Maryland of 1812 might have been called a swing state in modern parlance. Republicans controlled the majority of state offices, but Federalists had recently enjoyed an upsurge in support and remained competitive in the southern counties and along the Eastern Shore.[3]

Explosive growth brought growing prosperity to the city but also unrest and upheaval. Baltimore was becoming an unruly boomtown, and by the summer of 1812, this chunky stew of class, ethnic and religious division was nearing a flash point. If the city could be described as a powder keg, the man arguably most responsible for lighting the match was an unlikely protagonist.

"Firm in His Convictions, Fluent in Speech"

A man once described as "firm in his convictions, fluent in speech, of fine address and manner,"[4] Alexander Contee Hanson Jr. was born in the winter of 1786 in Annapolis, Maryland, the second son of a prominent Episcopalian family. Hanson's father was known to be a deeply religious man—one story recounts that he originally embarked on a career in the priesthood only to have his voyage to England interrupted by a shipwreck.[5] The younger Hanson's piety is less well known but what is clear is that he was a fierce devotee of Federalism.

Growing up in a Federalist family, Alexander Hanson developed an aversion to France as a boy reading accounts of the Reign of Terror during the French Revolution.[6] One such publication, "Bloody Buoy," depicted the French revolutionaries as barbarous and bloodthirsty cannibals—describing "women roasted alive, and their flesh cut off and presented to men for food."[7] These lurid accounts had an impact on young Hanson, and his hostility toward France would inform his views the rest of his life.

After completing his studies at St. John's College, Hanson practiced law for several years before launching his newspaper, the *Federal Republican and Commercial Gazette*, in 1808 at age twenty-two. The newspaper quickly earned a reputation as one of the nation's most extreme Federalist publications. Hanson himself developed the persona of a swashbuckling mudslinger who persisted and delighted in tormenting his Republican adversaries.

Hanson was known for his biting criticisms, and not all his targets accepted

Alexander Hanson, circa 1812. *From The Pictorial Field-book of the War of 1812.*

Left: Hanson's father, Alexander Contee Hanson Sr., served with George Washington and later became chancellor of Maryland, the state's highest-ranking judicial office. *Library of Congress*.

Right: Hanson's paternal grandfather, John Hanson, was a Revolutionary War officer who served in the Continental Congress and was later elected president of the United States in 1781 under the Articles of Confederation, the weaker predecessor of our U.S. Constitution. While his ceremonial title was "President of the United States in Congress assembled," John Hanson's function was more akin to a Speaker of the House than a chief executive. *Library of Congress*.

them well. A young naval officer named Charles Gordon discovered that Hanson's pointed barbs were not the only thing the Federalist newspaper editor was capable of firing. Gordon had the misfortune of serving as captain of the USS *Chesapeake* when the navy frigate was caught unprepared and forced to surrender to a British warship off the coast of Virginia in June 1807. The incident helped precipitate a trade embargo against Great Britain, and Gordon was reprimanded. Hanson penned a disparaging column in his newspaper about those involved in the *Chesapeake* debacle, and the criticism lingered with Gordon. Upon his next voyage to Baltimore, some eighteen months later, he challenged Hanson to a duel.[8]

The men met at noon on January 10, 1810, on a secluded field in Bladensburg, Maryland, just outside the District of Columbia line. Protected by dense trees and the banks of a rippling creek, the spot had become popular for duels since the seat of government had moved to Washington at the turn of the century. If Gordon, the veteran navy officer and experienced dueler, assumed his Federalist foe was just another

FEDERAL REPUBLICAN, & COMMERCIAL GAZETTE.

VOL. I.] MONDAY MORNING, JULY 4, 1808. [NO. I.

The price of this paper is 7 Dollars per annum, payable half yearly......Country subscribers must pay in advance.

PROPOSALS

For Publishing a new Morning Paper,

TO BE CALLED THE

FEDERAL REPUBLICAN,

AND

Commercial Gazette.

BY AN ASSOCIATION.

WHEN we reflect upon the critical situation of our country, a mingled sensation of gloomy apprehension and enlivening hope arises in the mind. The patriotic bosom is agonised with grief for the present and anxiety for the future... The general gloom which hangs over our afflicted country has broken the spirit and crushed the enterprize of a great people. Already we are sinking under our afflictions, but their measure is not filled. The evils we *may* have to encounter are sufficient to appal the stoutest hearts...Standing amidst the ruins of states and empires...spectators of the sad events, which in a "long, unbroken, funeral train," have passed in review before us, we are alarmed into reflection, our minds are purified by terror and pity; our weak, unthinking pride is humbled before the dispensations of a mysterious wisdom... The mound which stands between us and destruction, bends beneath the mighty, continued and accumulative force. Already we see the torrent, which has desolated Europe, approaching our hitherto peaceful and happy land.

It is the part of magnanimity to rise under the pressure of calamity...It is the attribute of prudence to anticipate future and to provide against impending evils... It might have been expected, that the freemen of America would be at last weary of humiliation and disgrace. It might have been expected, that a generous despair would rouse the spirit of enthusiasm, and that the electric spark would communicate its influence from Georgia to Maine. Such were our reasonable hopes, but they have not been gratified.

To meet the dangers which threaten to assail us, we have neither an army, nor a navy, nor fortifications. Political prejudice is opposed to an army; an exhausted treasury will not support a navy; and the plan of fortifications is incompatible with the system of economy. We have indeed *miniatures* of each, curious in appearance, but utterly insufficient for the purposes of national defence. The small military force, which our representatives have thought adequate to that important object, is placed under the command of a treacherous, and mercenary and hollow-hearted pensioner. A man suspected upon reasonable grounds to have been concerned in a traitorous conspiracy, whose brightest service, as recorded, consits in having become an informer to gratify disappointed ambition and to protract an inglorious life...A general, whose courage is comprised in vapouring, whose military skill is discernable only in the art of being upon good terms with the enemy... who has lost the confidence of his country, and is despised while he is detested! Such is the man whom administration has not dared to dismiss from office; who, when our shores are invaded by the bloodhounds of revolutionary France, is to lead on brave Americans to be butchered in the field, or sold to the enemy.

Our navy, that infant Hercules, which in the honest anticipating pride of the country, was to strangle the serpents of Europe, miserably made up of a few score of *ferry-boats*, instead of resisting the piratical depredations of foreigners, is preying upon our own vessels and tyrannising over our own citizens. Instead of chasing before them the French marauders who infest our ports, they are employed in enforcing unconstitutional decrees and orders...feeble, against our enemies, but formidable to us.

In our administration we behold the same blind confidence, improvident security, and servile submission, which, more than the arms of France, have subjected Europe to the yoke of the conqueror....

The proud aspiring spirit of Americans languishes under the effects of a mean, and dastardly, and degrading policy, which, while it humbles and impoverishes the nation, exposes it to scorn, contempt, and perpetual insult. The honor of a glorious people, who but a few years past humbled the pride of a mighty nation, is tarnished; the laurels, purchased by illustrious deeds of valor, have withered in the unhallowed and treacherous keeping of false patriots. The national spirit is mouldering away, the love of glory is giving place to the love of wealth, and all these evils are derived from the influence of a fatal system of expedients and of false economy.

A new period in our history is arrived. The principles, upon which parties divided at the formation of our Federal Constitution, have become of secondary consequence. We are not at this time contending for favorite theories. The question does not concern speculative points of government...it is more momentous, for it involves our eventual existence as freemen...It is to be determined whether we shall live under the government of our choice; or become the province of a foreign power; whether we shall exchange the garb of freemen for the livery of vassals..."An unseen hand" directs the councils of our country and urges us on to fatal ruin! With fear and trembling, we gaze on the black clouds which are rising above our political horizon, the distant thunder warns us of the approaching storm, whilst we, riveted by a fatal fascination, seek no shelter from the fury of the tempest. The roaring cannon of the enemy is pointed towards us, and we want the courage to defend ourselves.

Such is the most important feature in the face of our political affairs. But while one enemy assails us without, another is labouring within. A fixed determination has been betrayed by the party in power, to carry into operation a favourite theory of their leader...the annihilation of commerce. To further this purpose, the Constitution has been violated, power has been usurped, and the most perfect indifference to the sacred rights of the citizen has been manifested. A powerful party is arrayed in open hostility to the judiciary; a plan has been avowed and is ripe for execution, to cut away this great political anchor, at which, in the stormy times of peril and dismay, the vessel of state has rode in safety.

A lambent ray of hope gilds this dreary prospect. Our situation, though critical, is far from desperate...Wisdom points out a path to certain security. To pursue this path, the people must have virtue, fortitude and courage. They must no longer close their eyes to the dangers that threaten them. They must no longer blindly confide in their favourites. Would the people be sensible to their true situation, they may be yet rescued from the danger which awaits them; they may be saved from the common grave in which the liberties of Europe have been entombed, and slavery and wretchedness may not be entailed upon their posterity... Let us with grateful hearts render thanks to the supreme disposer of good and of evil, that symptoms of recovery are already visible, that the languishing body politic has had strength to contend with the raging fever which threatened to consume it, and for the hope that the struggles of nature will destroy the humours of disease. Once in a state of convalescence, we do not fear a relapse. The people will awake from the disturbed dreams of democratic philosophy, and, shaking off the administration, which sits like *incubus* upon them, will arise in the majesty of a great and magnanimous nation, will defend their rights with vigour and courage, and teach tyrants to respect their virtue.

If ever there was a time which demanded the exertions of those who love their country, it is the present. Much is to be apprehended and much to be hoped. But to realize our hopes the most indefatigable exertions are required from the friends of civil liberty and social order, from all classes of citizens, from the statesman, the scholar, and the soldier. Our enemies are active and persevering and our dearest interests are at stake. To give an exaggerated description of our difficulties and dangers is impossible. The most highly coloured fiction could not equal the reality. In vain are intrigue and artifice employed to lull us into security...our feelings tell us we are insulted and betrayed.

Alive to the distress and danger of our country, and influenced by a desire to contribute whatever aid it may be in our power to afford the American cause, we have determined to establish a New Journal to co-operate with those whose views are single to their country's good.

In the conduct of this paper we shall be regulated by the sound and healthful principles of the Federal school. We are not the disciples of Condorcet or of Paine. If our political tenets should ever want a further elucidation, we shall not call on democracy to explain them. We shall not light up our temple from that unhallowed fire. It will be illuminated with the rays of a more pure and lasting light. It will be perfumed with the incense of the memory of a WASHINGTON and a HAMILTON. Supporting the Federal Constitution, we shall cleave closely to the institutions of our ancestors, and viewing all innovation with a jealous eye, we shall mock at those miserable jugglers who have made a philosophy and a religion of their hostility to all order and all establishment.

Need we add any thing as to the moral and religious principles which our paper will ever inculcate and support? Knowing that religion is the basis of civil society, the source of all good and of all consolation, we will fight under its sacred banner to the last gasp; and stripping the impious and the infidel, the atheist and the deist of this false and deceitful garb, we will exhibit the monster in his native deformity.

To the mere student who devotes his time to literary acquirements, we may promise some relief from the ruggedness of politics and the asperities of controversial discussion. Passing "from grave to gay, from lively to severe," we shall endeavour to present a banquet for every taste. Interesting biographies, critical notices of new works, original and selected poetry will sometimes adorn our columns.

As much of the time and attention of its conductors will necessarily be consumed in rendering this establishment deserving of general approbation and support, it is at least desirable, that they should be secured in those pecuniary advances which are incident to it. They ask no more. Their object is not gain: they have higher and more honourable views. The disinterested motives, which have prompted them to this laborious undertaking, certainly give them a claim upon their political friends for favour and support. We confidently trust, that their independence and patriotism will urge them to aid us in an effort to serve our country.

To our commercial friends we would particularly address ourselves:...

"Gentle breath of theirs our sails
"Must fill, or else our project fails."

Their patronage is necessary to our existence; without it we must abandon all exertion. We shall offer them in return the closest attention to their interest, and our industrious efforts to procure the earliest mercantile intelligence. We cherish a hope, that they will not neglect us, but, by presenting us with a portion of their favours, preserve our exertions from the blasting influence of pecuniary embarrassment.

As to the manner of conducting our paper enough has been said. We will merely add, that the columns of the FEDERAL REPUBLICAN will be forever closed against scurrility and abuse. Manly and independent investigation into the actions of public men we earnestly invite... With equal caution we shall avoid the charge of virulence or of timidity; the characters of private citizens shall be preserved sacred and inviolable; but we will not wink at corruption in office, nor fear to express the indignation we feel against the foreign or domestic enemies of our country. In a word, we shall be directed by truth and patriotism; we shall endeavour to disseminate correct principles of government, to infuse into the public mind the love of glory, and to rouse the dormant spirit of America.

—

This paper will be published every morning, at the rate of $7 to annual subscribers, payable half yearly.

A Country Paper will be issued three times a week, at $5 per annum, payable in advance.

Advertisements will be inserted on the usual terms.

FOR SALE,

A large, able bodied bay Horse,

That goes well under the saddle, and is esteemed an excellent gig horse.—For terms apply at this Office.

July 4. eo6t

Fresh Teas.

The Subscribers are now ready to supply their friends and customers with fresh TEAS of every description, which they will warrant equal to any ever imported into the United States; they have been selected with the greatest attention from the cargoes of the Baltimore East India Company's ship William Bingham, in this city, and of the Mercury, and Pennsylvania Packet, in Philadelphia,

CONSISTING OF

51 chests, 10 boxes and 500 cannisters Imperial Tea,

15 chests and 20 boxes Hyson do.

15 chests and 20 boxes Young Hyson do.

4 chests Souchong Tea, of a very superior quality, for family use.

4 chests common do.

10 chests and 15 boxes Hyson skin do.

Just Received,

50 baskets [12 large bottles each] very superior sallad Oil.

30 boxes fresh Olives, Capers and Anchovies.

20 Bags and 2 hhds. soft shelled Almonds.

5 boxes [8 dozen each] first quality London Mustard.

Double Gloucester & Cheshire Cheese

A fresh supply of basket salt, &c. &c.

On Hand,

Genuine old Madeira and Port Wine, in casks and bottles.

Real Cogniac Brandy, 10 years old.

Old Jamaica spirits.

With a general assortment of Liquors and Groceries, &c. &c.

WHELAN & LAURENSON.

No. 132, Market-street.

July 4. 2aw4w

NOTICE.

Baltimore Water Company.

The President and Directors of the Water Company, considering the necessity of regular and prompt payment, to enable them to comply with their own engagements, which are all for ready money; the loss and delay that has already and must hereafter occur by death or other accidents where credit is given, and the great difficulty and expence of collecting where the transactions are so numerous, have

RESOLVED,

That all water rents must be paid half yearly in advance, on the first day of July and the first day of January, at the office of the Water Company.

That no deduction in water rent can be allowed when the water is stopped in the pipes or conduit, for the purpose of repairs, alterations, &c. unless the stoppage exceeds three days at any one period.

Every person on applying for water must pay in advance the sum of ten dollars; whenever the supply pipe is laid, and an account of the expences thereof and the water rent up to the next half yearly day of payment is furnished, payment must be made of the balance at the Company's office, within three days after the said account is thus furnished, under the penalty of the stoppage of the water and the loss of the ten dollars advanced, and the company must have the liberty to enter into the premises, take up and remove, if they choose to do so, all pipes, etc.

No person who is or shall be supplied with water, is on any account to admit water to be drawn and carried from their pipes or hydrant for any purpose except for the use of their own families, nor wilfully to draw and waste the water, under the penalty of having the supply stopped, which cannot again be returned without a new application to the company, and the payment of a fine of five dollars at the time of applying.

If any rented house supplied with water, should at any time for a period not less than three months, be vacant and not occupied, the owner, by giving a statement of the same to the office of the company, shall have the amount of the rent deducted, during the said period. All owners of property must be accountable to the company for water rent, and not the tenant.

By order of the Board,

SAMUEL A. CHEW, *Sec'ry.*

July 4.

General Lottery Office.

No 130, Market Street.

The subscribers beg leave to inform their friends and the public, that they have now now on hand, a large choice of numbers in the following Rich Lotteries, viz.

Charitable Marine,

Baltimore College,

Trinity Church,

Which they offer for sale at original prices, in whole, half, quarters and eighths.

The drawing of the CHARITABLE MARINE LOTTERY will positively commence on the 24th of next month, and will be completed in the short space of Ten Weeks.

We have yet remaining on hand a few Tickets in the Lottery for the ENCOURAGEMENT of USEFUL ARTS, *now drawing.*

Scheme.

CASH PRIZES.

1 prize of	10,000 dollars		10,000
2 do. of	5,000		10,000
5 do. of	1,000		5,000
10 do. of	500		5,000
10 do. of	200		2,000
40 do. of	100		4,000
100 do. of	50		5,000
200 do. of	20		4,000
300 do. of	10		3,000
1000 do.	To consist of machines for opening off cast worsted and open wrought woolen clothing into wool valued at 100 dolls. each, (patent right included)		100,000
1000 do.	To consist of rights for manufacturing ornamental mouldings for dwelling houses and shipping, valued at 50 dollars each,		50,000
			$200,000

Subject to a deduction of 15 per cent.

After the next day's drawing, the price of Tickets will be advanced to two Dollars.

This Lottery will be completed in 18 days drawing after the 5th inst.

Prizes in other Lotteries taken in exchange, and *all* Tickets examined gratis.

*** Adventurers at a distance inclosing the money (post paid) will be attended to, and the earliest information given them as to the fate of their Tickets.

P. Byrne, Sen'r. & *Sutherland*.

July 4. tf

Baltimore and Reisters' town Turnpike Road Company.

The President and Managers of this Company require the payment of a fourth being the last instalment of Five Dollars on each share of the augmented stock, on Thursday, the 1st day of September next, at the Bank of Baltimore.

By order,

JOHN F. HARRIS, *Sec'ry.*

July 4. t1S

John H. Ross,

No. 55, St. Patrick's Row, Market Space,

Having obtained letters patent from the president of the United States, for *Convex Illuminators*, calculated to light ships' cabins, state rooms, stair cases, closets, work shops, or any other apartment requiring light, solicits the orders of his friends and the public.

The great advantage of these *Illuminators* must be obvious: They are so solid as not to be broken, but by the greatest violence, and may have casks or other bodies rolled over them without injury: they can with great convenience be placed in the deck on the dead lights, or ports of vessels, as to afford a good light in the worst weather, and may be rendered perfectly water tight, and moveable at pleasure.

To the artist or mechanic, they will afford a strong and steady light, without the glare so distressing to the eyes...and upon the whole, will be found eminently useful in a great variety of situations and for various purposes.

J. H. Ross takes this opportunity of recommending to the attention of the public, his *Patent Water Closets*, acting upon a simple and improved principle. They are constructed so as to exclude all disagreeable effluvia, and may be fixed in dressing rooms, bed chambers, or any other part of the house. They are not liable to accidents from bursting of pipes, occasioned by frost or other causes.

He also constructs and fixes a great variety of lifting and forced pumps, for the purpose of raising water to any height required, or conveying it to any distance, calculated to save labor in brewhouses, sugar houses, distilleries, &c.

Also, air traps for sinks, drains, or other inlets to sewers, by which all houses may be rendered perfectly sweet at a very trifling expence.

House and Ship Plumber's work, well executed, in the best manner; and Hatter's Kettles at the shortest notice.

July 4. 2awif

Post-Office,

Baltimore, June 20, 1808.

The public are hereby informed, that the mail for Chambersburg direct, will in future be closed at this office every Tuesday and Saturday at 5 o'clock, P. M. Will arrive every Monday and Thursday at 7 o'clock, P. M.

Charles Burrall,

Above: While not officially sanctioned, dueling was still an accepted custom to settle political scores, even after the death of Alexander Hamilton in a duel with Aaron Burr some five years prior in New York. *Library of Congress.*

Opposite: The first issue of the *Federal Republican and Commercial Gazette* was published on July 4, 1808. The following year, Hanson partnered with the *North American and Mercantile Daily Advertiser* published by Jacob Wagner. The newly merged publication kept the *Federal Republican* name with Wagner serving as co-editor. *From the* Federal Republican.

avuncular newspaper editor, he was mistaken. Hanson, despite being frail and often in ill-health, had grown up on a plantation, served in the local militia and was an experienced shot.

Pistols in hand, the two men marched off five paces and turned to each other. Gordon was slow to lift his weapon from his left arm (there are conflicting reports whether Gordon fumbled with his pistol or fired in the air), while Hanson, with "marvelous coolness and nonchalance," got off a shot quickly.[9] His aim was true, and Gordon was struck in the abdomen, above his right hipbone. He fell to the ground. The wound was severe and initially reported as fatal, but Gordon survived, though the wound left him disabled and his run-in with Hanson would shadow him the rest of his life.[10]

The fallout from Hanson's broadsides against the British trade embargo continued. Maryland's Republican governor ordered a court-martial against Hanson for a column he wrote in his November 30, 1808 edition, alleging it was "mutinous and highly reproachful." Hanson, a lieutenant in the Maryland Militia's Thirty-Ninth Regiment, was hauled in for a court-martial hearing where he vigorously defended his actions in written testimony and offered up an eloquent treatise on the freedom of the press.[11] The judge advocate hearing the case ruled in Hanson's favor.

The pattern was becoming clear. Somewhat like the porcupines that inhabited the woods near Hanson's family estate, the newspaper editor was adept with the quill, full of pointed barbs and could get prickly when attacked.

THE FATEFUL HEADLINE

Thou has done a deed, whereat valor will weep. Without funds, without taxes, without an army, navy, or adequate fortifications…our rulers have promulgated a war against the clear and decided sentiments of a vast majority of the nation.
—Federal Republican, *Saturday, June 20, 1812*

Thus began the fateful column in Saturday's edition of the *Federal Republican*. The march toward war with Great Britain had provided plenty of editorial fodder for the fiery Federalist newspaper editor to engage and enrage the Baltimore populace, and now, with the official declaration of war two days prior, Hanson was ready to unload on President Madison and his fellow Republicans.

What followed in the editorial was a pointed and partisan deconstruction of an "impolitic and destructive war," which Hanson believed was opposed by the majority of Americans. Rather than dwell in the "dreadful detail" of the impending conflict, the editorial charted a course of opposition, calling on countrymen to resist "till we sink with the liberty of our country, or sink alone." Lest there be any doubt as to whom the Hanson blamed for pulling the administration's strings, the editorial invoked the French emperor himself: "We are avowedly hostile to the presidency of James Madison, and we will never breathe under the dominion or directive of Bonaparte."

Word of this latest Federalist treachery spread quickly. On Sunday afternoon, crowds met in locations around Baltimore to plot revenge. Many

APPROVED, JAMES MADISON.
On the final passage of the Act in the Senate. the vote was 19 to 13 ; in the House 79 to 49.

BALTIMORE

SATURDAY, JUNE 20.

" *Thou has done a deed, whereat valor will weep.*"

Without funds, without taxes, without an army, navy, or adequate fortifications, with one hundred and fifty millions of our property in the hands of the declared enemy, without any of his in our power, and with a vast commerce afloat, our rulers have promulged a war, against the clear and decided sentiments of a vast majority of the nation. As the consequences will be so soon felt, there is no need of pointing them out to the few, who have not sagacity enough to apprehend them. Instead of employing our pen in this dreadful detail, we think it more apposite to delineate the course we are determined to pursue, as long as the war shall last. We mean to represent in as strong colors as we are capable, that it is unnecessary, inexpedient, and entered into from partial, personal, and as we believe, motives bearing upon their front marks of undisguised foreign influence, which cannot be mistaken.— We mean to use every constitutional argument and every legal means to render as odious and suspicious to the American people, as they deserve to be, the patrons and contrivers of this high

ris in the bloody days of Robespierre. Let them but suffer one or two more examples of a mob's usurpation, and individuals will cease to look for protection to any other shield than their own strength, or by crouching in slavish submission; & they will thereafter find their lives their property at the disposal of a banditti, whose authority will be founded upon terror, and whose maxims in executing their ferocious decrees will be derived from a diabolical excess of the worst passions which sway the human heart.

We have not the remotest idea, that the scandalous doctrines of the National Intelligencer and its auxiliaries, have obtained a footing in this state except with an insignificant few, whose ignorance and want of reflection are upon a par with their malignity. But were any irregularity for a moment to break out here, it would be met in a manner, which would do honor to the spirit and enlightened patriotism of the citizens. Those who should dare to disturb public order would be the only and certain victims of the attempt.— For men are not yet prepared to regard Madison and his partizans as possessing the standard of opinion, either for federalists or democrats, and it will not be tolerated, that his minions should create themselves into revolutionary tribunals to ascertain, who shall wear his head or enjoy his property any longer.

The editorial in the June 10, 1812 issue took fewer than 450 words, but the impact was immediate. See appendix for full text. *From the* Federal Republican.

gathered at Pamphilion's Hotel in Fell's Point near the shipyards. Another meeting was held at a nearby public garden, where a plan was hatched to destroy the newspaper office and silence the editors. According to a witness at one of the meetings, nearly three hundred men signed a pact to assist one another in the execution of their attack.

News of an orchestrated uprising against the newspaper leaked out quickly, but Hanson, who rarely shied from any kind of fight, did not appear to take the threat too seriously; in the Republican bastion of Baltimore, the pro-Federalist iconoclast was conditioned to abuse. Hanson wasn't in the city at the time, but rather back home in Montgomery County, a day's horse ride away. He and a cadre of likeminded Federalists were meeting at a local tavern in Unity, a village in the northeast end of Montgomery County, but there was no talk of unity on their agenda this evening. The men were meeting to draft resolutions condemning the new war and the Republican leadership in Congress.[12]

Back in Baltimore, Jacob Wagner, Hanson's partner, was more concerned by the growing unrest, so he decided to take the precaution of taking the company books out of the office. It was around "early candle light" on Monday when Wagner walked from his house over to the newspaper office at the corner of Gay and Second Streets in the heart of Old Town. The streets were illuminated by oil lamp; gas-powered lights were several years off. He likely walked past the German Reformed Church, where sermons were still given in German for the city's large immigrant population.[13] As he retrieved his papers and proof sheet for the next morning's edition, Wagner was joined by a friend. The pair left the office and walked a short distance to stop in at the home of a third man a few blocks away.

Wagner didn't know it at the time, but that visit probably saved his life.

2

THE FIRST ATTACK

That house is the Temple of Infamy.

BALTIMORE, JUNE 22, 1812—At first it was just a few boys throwing stones—then came the axes, ropes and fire hooks. Between eight and nine o'clock on a clear Monday evening, the mob began gathering around the office of the *Federal Republican* newspaper. They were local shopkeepers, craftsmen, merchant sailors and recent immigrants from Old Town and neighboring Fell's Point. The moon was nearly full.

After breaking the front locks, the men formed a double line encircling the newspaper office and commenced a loosely orchestrated process of tearing down the two-story wood-framed building. About thirty men actively joined in the demolition, while a larger crowd of spectators grew around the building as news spread. The ringleader was Dr. Philip Lewis, a Frenchman who was no doctor at all, just a local apothecary who had immigrated to Baltimore. Little is known about his bedside manner, but several witnesses would later testify to the Frenchman's violent tendencies.

Baltimore mayor Edward Johnson was drinking tea at the home of a neighbor that evening. Intending to retire for the night, he walked back to his home on King George Street around 8:30 p.m. and was about to open his front door when he was first told of the disturbance at the newspaper office. Johnson, the son of a well-known physician and former state assemblyman, was a doctor himself and a popular figure in the city.

Edward Johnson was just the third mayor in Baltimore's history, first winning election in 1808. Johnson operated a large and successful brewery near his home but soon found the demands of brewing, medicine and politicking too much, and he sold the brewery in 1813. Later that year, a local flag maker used one of the brewery's malt houses to sew the finishing touches on a massive American flag that then flew from Fort Henry and inspired "The Star-Spangled Banner." *Maryland Historical Society.*

After hearing the news, Mayor Johnson returned to his neighbor's house to convince his reluctant friend to accompany him, and the two men began walking toward the melee. They crossed the double bridge over the Jones Falls and walked past the mills to the Centre Markets, where the aroma of tobacco and roasting coffee often filled the air.[14] When they reached the intersection of Frederick Street, a few blocks from the scene of the mob, another friend stopped them and advised the mayor to return home, saying the damage was already done. "He was confident there would be no further mischief," the mayor later recounted.

Mayor Johnson decided to heed that advice and retreated to King George Street with his neighbor. It is not known whether he was truly convinced the danger had passed or just reluctanct to insert himself into a conflict pitting his own Republican supporters against a despised Federalist newspaper. It's likely that Mayor Johnson was at least generally aware that an attack had been planned the day before, though he did later deny having any specific knowledge.

Around the same time, two men who had been at the scene of the attack on the newspaper office, John Worthington and Samuel Hollingsworth, began walking to the mayor's house to seek help. The men all crossed paths by the brewery near the mayor's home. Worthington and Hollingsworth recounted the violent scene they had just witnessed and believed that a small show of force could convince the mob to stand down and restore order in the city.

"Give me twenty horse and I will disperse the scoundrels—yes, sir, give me twelve and I will do it!" Hollingsworth said as the small group stood along King George Street. The mayor replied that he had no power to do so. During the conversation, two of the mayor's political allies—who had also returned from the mob scene—joined him. They both urged the mayor not to interfere.

"Mr. Johnson I advise you not to go; you cannot prevent it, and without support may expose yourself to great personal risk," said one neighbor.

But Worthington persisted and pressed the mayor. "Then sir, accompany us to the mob, let us endeavor to find out the ringleader—let us make some effort to save the property and lives of our fellow-citizens," he said. His colleague Hollingsworth threatened to go to a local magistrate if the mayor did not take action.

"Gentlemen, I will risk my life with the mayor if he will go," Hollingsworth added.

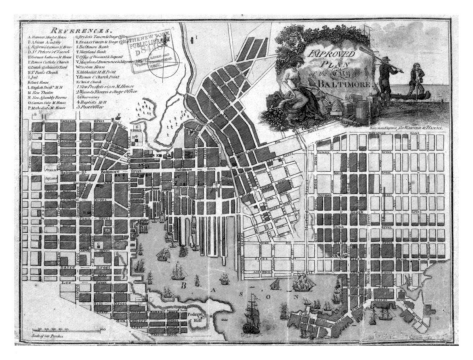

The newspaper office was located at the corner of Gay and Second Streets in the Old Town section of Baltimore. Warner & Hanna map circa 1804. *New York Public Library.*

The mayor was clearly torn between the two factions. Here the various accounts diverge. According to Hollingsworth, the mayor finally relented only because he agreed to accompany him back to the mob scene. The mayor saw events differently and recalled that he voluntarily offered to go at his own risk even against the wisdom of his own supporters. In either case, the mayor took Hollingsworth by the arm, and along with Worthington, the men walked back toward Gay Street, where the mob was still in the process of tearing down the newspaper building with ropes and fire hooks. When they arrived, the crowd of spectators had grown larger.

"The Mayor, the mayor, make room for the mayor!" Hollingsworth exclaimed, pushing through the scrum of angry rioters. The men slowly made their way to the center of the crowd, where they encountered Dr. Lewis, the French apothecary and violent ringleader of the mob. The mayor addressed the crowd, reminding them that such lawlessness would be punished.

"You say your object is to destroy the *Federal Republican*; you are now not doing that, you are destroying the property of an innocent man," the mayor told the crowd, according to one eyewitness.

Worthington saw the conversation differently. "My impression was that the mayor did not make a proper effort to be heard—he observed in a low and faltering tone to one, 'my dear fellow, you ought not to do so'—and to another, 'my dear fellow, you do not know the consequences of what you are doing.'"

It probably did not matter. While Dr. Lewis and Mayor Johnson may have been on the same side of the political fence, the Frenchman was not interested in negotiation on this evening.

"Mr. Johnson, I know you very well, nobody wants to hurt you; but the laws of the land must sleep, and the laws of nature and reason must prevail," the Frenchman said, summing up the feelings of many in the crowd.

"That house is the Temple of Infamy," he continued, pointing to the newspaper office, "it is supported with English gold, and it must and shall come down to the ground!" After making his comments, the Frenchman turned away from the mayor, seized a rope and cried out, "Huzza boys, down with it, pull away!"

"RAPID DESCENT UPON BRITISH POSSESSIONS."—*P. B. PORTER.*

While Hanson's June 20 editorial was the latest provocation, there was no shortage of material to rile up local residents, including this political cartoon mocking President Madison earlier in the year. An accompanying article referred to Madison, depicted as a monkey, as "the little man in the white house." *From the* Federal Republican.

Dr. Philip Lewis and several others were later charged with unlawful assembly and "riotously aiding" in the destruction of the Federal Republican newspaper office. In a later jury trial, they were found not guilty. *Maryland State Archives.*

Unable to quell the disturbance and sensing the futility of his words, the mayor soon departed to get help with Hollingsworth in tow. Worthington was less fortunate. He somehow became separated in the crowd and, for a few tense moments, found himself alone amid the rioters.

"Who are you, sir? What business have you here?" the angry Frenchman confronted Worthington after noting his presence.

"A spy—a spy!" came from the cry from the crowd.

Worthington later described the scene, "I was surrounded by the mob, with axes, clubs and fists, suspended over my head, with a cry of 'make him take hold of the rope or down with him.'" With some deception, Worthington managed to elude the crowd and make his escape, and the rioters returned to their original prey.

RIOTERS ON THE RAMPAGE

The destruction of the *Federal Republican* office continued well into the night. The building slowly came down, and the presses, printing apparatus, type, books and papers were thrown out of the house, scattered and destroyed. The building itself was leveled to the foundation. With crowd estimates ranging from three hundred to up to one thousand, the scene may have been chaotic, but witnesses described the demolition as organized and "performed with great regularity." One unfortunate attacker attempted to knock out a window on the upper floor, fell with it onto the street and was killed—breaking two ribs of an unlucky bystander in the process.

Emboldened by their success destroying the newspaper office and perhaps frustrated by the absence of Hanson and his coeditor Wagner, the rioters searched out their next target. Believing that one might be hiding in the bank building across the street from the printing office, the mob gathered outside the steps sometime after midnight. They pressed forward toward the doors and demanded Wagner be released.

While some of the city's leading Republican citizens may have felt ambivalence or even pleasure at the mob's retaliation against perceived Federalist infidelity, others rose to the occasion. Two respected citizens, Dr. John Owen and Andrew Boyd, anticipated the mob moving on to the bank, or the Baltimore Office of Discount and Deposit as it was known, and attempted to intercede. The pair met up with a band of rioters at the back stairs in an effort to prevent more destruction.

"We continued to pledge ourselves, as known Republicans, and whose word of honour ought not to be treated with contempt...that Wagner was not in the house," Dr. Owen told the mob leaders. The effort apparently worked, and after a short time, the crowd dispersed without further damage to the building. "I have no doubt the doors would have been forced, and the house examined, if it was not for the handsome conduct of the above mentioned gentlemen," one witness later recounted.

Momentarily dissuaded, the mob was still not ready to go gently. Nor would it be so easily rebuffed at their next stop. Wagner's father-in-law lived nearby on Water Street. He wasn't home that evening, but Wagner's wife was. Her brother, Christopher Raborg, a local brass maker, heard rumblings and feared an attack, so he rushed over to protect his sister.

It was some time before two o'clock in the morning when Raborg arrived, finding the Water Street home surrounded, with several men trying to get in the locked front door. The assembled mob knocked violently and demanded to search the house, believing Hanson's partner to still be inside. Raborg himself was roughed up, grabbed by the collar and "threatened with a suit of tar and feathers."

Mrs. Wagner finally opened the door and bravely addressed the men, gently touching the arm of the lead ruffian. "Gentlemen, enter and search, I will go before you with a light, you will find none but females," she said.

After some tense moments a pair of the mob leaders—one a "new imported Irishman"—were allowed to enter and conduct a search. The men were thorough and searched the house from top to bottom, even attempting to cut open the beds. The search ended with no sign of Wagner or Hanson, and the mob's frustration was rising. An argument ensued about what to do next and then a fight broke out in front of the house. Eventually, the mob moved on and decided to search Wagner's own house on Charles Street for a second time.

It was the middle of the night, and Wagner's next-door neighbor was sleeping when he heard the thumping at a door. He looked out his window and saw a group of men gathering outside at his neighbor's house, demanding to know where to find "Wagner, the Tory printer." The men made several unsuccessful attempts to force open Wagner's front door and then managed to get in the yard through a gate. A "negro servant" who was inside the house and alarmed by the attacks quickly departed and, in his haste, left open a kitchen door with a candle burning. The light drew the attention of the mob—as well as Christopher Raborg, who had just returned from his sister's house after learning about the latest disturbance.

Raborg had changed his clothes and must have thought he was not recognizable to this pack of rioters as he made his way into the yard in the midst of the crowd. Thinking quickly, Raborg, or perhaps one of his allies, paid a young boy to go to the yard next door and exclaim, "Here he goes, he has just leaped the fence!" The ploy worked, and the mob took off in hot pursuit of this red herring, armed with cudgels, sticks and whatever they could find in the yard. Raborg used the opportunity to secure all the windows and doors in Wagner's house.

He had now witnessed the mob in action on at least three separate occasions over the course of the evening, and the concerns for his friend Alexander Hanson and his brother-in-law Jacob Wagner were well placed. The rioters were bloodthirsty and relentless. Later, when asked about the mob's pursuit he remarked, "I am confident if they had succeeded in finding the object of their pursuit, his life would have been the forfeit."

The message was delivered even more clearly to Mrs. Wagner. After encountering one of the mob members later that evening back at her father's house, she asked if they intended to injure her husband should he be found. The reply was chilling: "Yes, the rascal, we would have blown a pistol through his heart."

View of Old Town from the harbor. *Library of Congress.*

It was nearly five o'clock in the morning on Tuesday when the sun began to rise in Baltimore. The rioters, running out of targets and darkness, eventually dispersed with no further bloodshed. Only one fatality was reported throughout the course of the night, but the mob had blazed a trail of terror and destruction that would not soon disappear. By Tuesday morning, the streets of Baltimore had cleared, but any sense of peace was illusory.

The mob had awoken, and it would be back.

3

CITY UNDER SIEGE

The boards and shingles flew so thick and violent,
that I could not get to the house.

ROCKVILLE, MARYLAND, C. JUNE 24, 1812—From his Rockville home in Montgomery County, Alexander Hanson learned of the mob's attack, the destruction of the newspaper office and the narrow escape of his partner. His friend John Howard Payne, an aspiring actor and songwriter, immediately wrote Hanson from Baltimore, advising him to stay away.

"I suggested, that under existing circumstances it would be imprudent and improper for him to visit Baltimore, without preconcerting some plan of defence," Payne recounted.

Others urged Hanson to rally his supporters and strike back. "Unless the people are immediately roused, and the Federalists are immediately rallied, all opposition to the ruling policy will be unnerved," Hanson's cousin John Hanson Thomas wrote shortly after the attack, "and the influence of these satanic outrages in Baltimore will spread through the State."

There was little chance of Hanson going away quietly. He had much invested in his newspaper—politically and financially. While he and his wife, Priscilla Dorsey Hanson, both hailed from prominent Maryland families, Hanson was not a wealthy man. He had borrowed money to help launch the newspaper, and many of his early letters to friends and business associates were requests for money or complaints about his creditors and loan terms.

John Howard Payne would later earn fame as a playwright and songwriter, best known for the ballad "Home Sweet Home." ("Mid pleasures and palaces, though we may roam; Be it ever so humble, there's no place like home.") The song was a favorite of both Union and Confederate soldiers during the Civil War, was played for a grieving President Lincoln after the death of his son and even made a cameo in *The Wizard of Oz*. Payne was posthumously inducted into the Songwriters Hall of Fame in 1970, 118 years after his death. *New York Public Library*.

Hanson was shy about asking to borrow money and knew his political enemies would use the fact against him. Shortly after his marriage, he wrote to a local attorney asking for a loan of $200 to $300, with the caveat that "should you find it out of your power to oblige me, you will be so good as not to mention my application to you as I do not wish it known."[15]

Although Priscilla was due to inherit part of her late father's sizable estate in Elkridge in several years, it was tied up in legal limbo. Her father, Edward Dorsey—known as "Iron-Head Ned" because he and his brother ran a family forge and ironworks on the Patapsco River—died when Priscilla was nine years old, and her mother just a few years later. She was sixteen and living with guardians in Baltimore when the brash young Hanson came courting. Her guardians must not have approved because they refused to consent to a marriage, but this proved only a temporary setback, as the headstrong young couple decided to elope.[16]

The drama following Hanson's career may have begun before his journey into marriage and literally on the journey itself. According to one account, on June 24, 1805, the young couple was rushing from Baltimore to Annapolis to elope when a pinwheel in their carriage wagon broke. However, the clever Hanson had the foresight to bring a spare pin and quickly solved the problem, thus allowing him and his bride to arrive in Annapolis, where Hanson's family lived, just in time for the marriage ceremony that evening.[17] Whether the story is true or not, it certainly reinforces what we know about Hanson, who could be both meticulous and impetuous. Both qualities would inform his next actions in response to the initial newspaper attack in Baltimore.

The words of caution from his friend John Howard Payne had the opposite effect on Hanson. The next day, he traveled back to Baltimore with another friend to survey the damage firsthand and assess the prospects for reestablishing the paper. The visit was later described in a deposition.

"Finding it impossible to render any service, the laws being effectually silenced," the men returned home after a short time. Hanson was determined not to let the mob muzzle him or his newspaper, and he vowed not return to Baltimore again until he was ready to vindicate his rights.

CHAOS REIGNS IN THE CITY

While Hanson commenced preparations in Montgomery County, disorder and chaos continued to reign in Baltimore. The violence had not ended with the destruction of the newspaper office on the night of June 22. Anti-Federalist mobs continued to roam the streets and lash out against anything even remotely pro-British or pro-Federalist—epithets that were redundant to most of the rioters.

The next day, the mob targeted a local innkeeper who allegedly made the mistake of offering a toast to "the health of King George and damnation to the Americans." A hostile crowd seeking to tar and feather him surrounded the man's house after sunset. This time, Mayor Johnson, who lived nearby, intervened more actively and helped the innkeeper escape through his backyard.

Down at the wharf in Fell's Point later that same evening, merchant vessels destined for British ports and in support of British allies in Spain

Baltimore town circa 1752 was a sleepy village. Poppleton Map. *Library of Congress*.

By the early nineteenth century, Baltimore had grown into a bustling seaport and the nation's third-largest city. Poppleton Map. *Library of Congress.*

and Portugal were vandalized. One ship dismantled by the mob was the *Dumfries*, advertised as a "Fast Sailing Ship" and bound for Lisbon with a cargo of flour. A Portuguese brig called the *Albuquerque* was also derigged and prevented from leaving port, and not even the packet ship *America*, with its cargo of flour and corn, was spared the mob's wrath.[18]

In Old Town, an Englishman who lived on Fish Street was attacked that week, reportedly because his sign read "From London." He told an official he avoided harm only by brandishing a gun and escaping in the confusion. Another man was forced to flee Baltimore after the rioters twice attacked his house and threatened him after reports surfaced that he said he hoped "the streets of Quebec would be paved with the bones of those troops who should march from the United States to attack Canada."

Some prominent Federalists felt Baltimore was no longer a safe place to be. James McHenry, a contemporary of Hanson's father and a former secretary of war, wrote to the owner of the newspaper building destroyed by the mob as he was leaving the city. A show of force was needed to restore peace, McHenry advised his friend, and warned "that the air of Baltimore is the air of a prison; that houses are no places of safety; that there is a mine under them ready to explode, the moment they shall either by word or by look, give offence to their masters."[19]

With those ominous words, McHenry, the elder statesman and signer of the U.S. Constitution, left the city and headed for his home in Allegany County. The star-shaped Fort McHenry overlooked Baltimore Harbor and protected the city but apparently could not protect the man it was named after.

While the reaction of Baltimore's city leaders was criticized in some parts, the mob activity certainly did capture their attention. The day after the initial

James McHenry. *Library of Congress.*

newspaper attack, Mayor Johnson sought out some of the city's leading residents to share news of the violence and express his concern. He called a meeting in his council chambers to solicit advice, later explaining his rationale: "Party spirit ran so high that a general armament would be resorted to, our city deluged with blood, and involved in all the horrors of civil war."

The mayor asked his advisors to research the law to determine what authority he had to call in the militia and was told it was limited to cases of invasion or insurrection. Whether the terms of the law were broad enough to apply to the present situation was the subject of debate. The mayor's advisors generally agreed he did have the authority, but one warned that the public did not always appreciate the "interference of the military with the civil authority." The mayor himself later voiced another rather chilling reason for not calling on the militia—their ranks were filled with the kind of men most prone to join the mob, he said.

A public town meeting to be held at the Centre Market on Wednesday afternoon was advertised in the morning newspapers, but it was postponed by the mayor due to heavy rain.[20] It is not clear if that public meeting was ever rescheduled, but a smaller meeting did take place at the mayor's office. There the mayor was joined by about thirty of the "most respectable of the city, and of both of the political descriptions, generally known as Republicans and Federalists," according to one resident.

The meeting with the mayor may have included a bipartisan crowd, but the sentiment in the room clearly ran against the Federalists and in support of the Republican mayor. One prominent attendee declared he would "cut the rascals ears off" if he heard pro-British expressions in person.

City leaders realized they would have to take more decisive action. At the town hall meeting, it was generally agreed that the mayor would issue a proclamation calling for peace and asking citizens to stand united in "discountenancing all irregular and tumultuous meetings." The notice ran in Thursday morning's city newspapers. Still, most of the men advising the mayor did not feel a military response was required.

Despite the efforts of city leaders, the violence continued. While the mob's initial thrust was to strike back against perceived Federalist perfidy, the violence escalated and grew more diffuse as the summer days wore on. Religious and racial antagonisms resurfaced as the disorganized rioters sought out more targets.

A Protestant Irish immigrant named Alexander Wiley who lived near the printing office was twice threatened by a mob (of mostly fellow Irishmen) and forced to flee his home under the pretext that he made deliveries for Hanson's newspaper. He did not, according to most reports, and Wiley told a militia leader the attacks were based on religious animosity.

Party politics may have provoked the rioting, but now many residents saw it devolving into historical grudge matches. "Neither Wiley himself, or any of the mob…seemed to understand much about political subjects, or the distinction of parties," one militia officer reported. "They had a cant term, 'Tory' which was the signal for insult and violence." In the coded language of political messaging, *Tory* was a useful and all-purpose insult.

Violence against African Americans also became a flashpoint. Baltimore had a sizeable minority population; in a city of approximately 46,000, African-Americans comprised 22 percent of the population. While Maryland was firmly a slave state, the population of free blacks in Baltimore was growing rapidly. In 1790, there were 1,623 slaves and fewer than 400 free black residents, according to the census. By the 1810 census, free blacks outnumbered slaves in the city. Baltimore had grown more ethnically diverse than other seaboard ports and less reliant on slave labor than its southern neighbors, but racial tensions remained, often driven by economic anxiety. Stuck between freedom and servitude, the city's free black residents often competed with the white working poor for jobs in the maritime or service industries.[21]

The simmering hostility bubbled to a boil in late June as the rioting expanded in chaotic fashion. One target was James Briscoe, a prominent free black resident who owned two or more houses in the city. Briscoe found himself in the mob's crosshairs after word circulated that he'd made pro-British statements (by one account) or voiced "threatening language about whites" (by another). The mob's rationale may have been cloaked more in racial prejudice than anti-Federalist zeal, but the result was the same: a group assembled in front of Briscoe's house in the Federal Hill neighborhood and began to attack, pulling down the building until the front of the house was entirely destroyed.

"The boards and shingles flew so thick and violent, that I could not get to the house," reported a local magistrate who arrived on the scene. The mob returned to Briscoe's property the next evening (mostly intoxicated, according to one witness) and this time targeted the adjoining building where Briscoe's daughter lived.

Briscoe may have been the most prominent African American targeted by the mob, but he was hardly the only victim. Numerous incidents of threats and attacks against the city's minority population were reported, sparking fears for potential retaliation.

"In the midst of all this anarchy and confusion, alarms were raised of a conspiracy among the negroes, hostile to the whites," wrote one militia captain, summarizing what was on the mind of some of Baltimore city leaders during their meeting with the mayor.

There is scant evidence to suggest any uprising was planned, but that did not prevent the mob from targeting the Sharp Street Methodist Church, a prominent gathering place for African Americans and a symbol of the city's growing free black population. Rumors of an attack against the church swirled, and the mob gathered for a confrontation. This time, city officials took decisive action, and the cavalry was dispatched, along with some "respectable Methodists," to quell the disturbance. No further violence was reported.

Daniel Coker, minister of the Sharp Street Congregation, was a leader in the African Methodist community and established one of the first schools for African American students. *New York Public Library*.

The show of force by city leaders represented a change in strategy from the initial reaction to the mob attack against Hanson's newspaper office. Gentle persuasion had given way to stronger tactics. The mayor acknowledged as much, stating that "the treatment received by the blacks, rendered it indispensable to adopt measures for their protection." Mayor Johnson's political skills would soon be tested in an even greater emergency. But first, the city paused for a rare moment of tranquility as the nation celebrated its National Jubilee.

FOURTH OF JULY CELEBRATION

The citizens of Baltimore awoke Saturday morning, July 4, to the sounds of cannons and bells ringing, but for the first time in nearly a fortnight, the gunfire that followed was only ceremonial. The city's festivities began with a tribute to George Washington in the Holliday Street Theatre and then a formal procession to Howard's Park, northwest of the city. "Yankee Doodle" played in the background as the mayor and fellow dignitaries gathered onstage before a sizeable crowd and, after opening prayers, heard a recitation of the Declaration of Independence. Levi Winder, a prominent Federalist political leader, gave an oration, which was reportedly well received even by the Republican-dominated crowd. Winder did not specifically mention the ongoing violence in the city but commented on the spirit of liberty, calling it "a fire not to be quenched, it demands a uniform vigilance to prevent its bursting into a flame; lest, instead of warming, it should consume."[22] The message was subtle but distinct.

Contemporary accounts in both the Federalist and Republican press emphasized the harmony of the day's events with many references to the bipartisan nature of the festivities. The Federalists even agreed to shift the time of their Washington tribute to accommodate the larger citywide procession. But if "concord and unanimity" were the mottos of the day, not all of Baltimore was listening.

In Fell's Point, the local Republican Party committee met at Pamphilion's Hotel for the neighborhood's Fourth of July celebration. After a "sumptuous" dinner, patrons joined in a series of toasts, which, as was often the practice, were later recounted in the local newspaper. Among the patriotic paeans were toasts to former president Jefferson, the army and navy and surviving patriots of the Revolution—all accompanied by music, cheers and gunfire salutes. Mixed in with the ceremonial gunshots were a few warning shots, including a toast to "unanimity among all citizens; may our internal foes meet their just reward," followed by a rendition of "Rogue's March," a traditional melody for criminals and dishonored soldiers. Another toast was raised to "the internal enemies of our country. May they be rapidly exported without benefit of drawback."[23]

Still, the nation's thirty-sixth birthday, with such a patriotic celebration of the Constitution, liberty and freedom, did offer the city a reprieve from nearly two straight weeks of violence—at least locally. The nation remained under declaration of war, and hostilities with Great Britain were heating up. It was just days later when Baltimore residents first learned of a planned attack by U.S. general William Hull against Canada, then a British colony. The attempted invasion was one of the first major military actions of the war.

Back in Montgomery County, Alexander Hanson was ready for an invasion of a different sort. He had spent the past few weeks plotting a return to Baltimore to revive his newspaper. Rather than dissuade or intimidate him, the mob violence had stiffened Hanson's resolve, and he vowed to defend the free press at any cost. The celebrated tenets of liberty and freedom were about to be put to the test—and this "war" was also just beginning.

4

PLOTTING AND PREPARATION

Water and biscuit be sure to have in abundance.

BALTIMORE, JULY 26, 1812—Alexander Hanson arrived in Baltimore on Sunday, a little more than a month after the mob had first silenced his newspaper, and this time he was ready for a fight. He'd spent his time in Montgomery County recruiting supporters and formulating a plan to relaunch the *Federal Republican* and prepare for the inevitable retaliation to follow. For Hanson, the act of defending his newspaper and triumphing over the mob represented a broader battle between liberty and tyranny; the freedom of the press was at stake, and he approached his crusade with growing fanaticism.

He departed his Rockville home on Friday with his wife, Priscilla, and his young children, Edward Pickering and Mary Rebecca. (The couple's firstborn, Alexander Contee Hanson III, is not mentioned and likely died at birth or in infancy.) Little Mary, about eighteen months old, was probably named after Hanson's sister, Mary, and his late mother, Rebecca. Three-year-old Edward, known as an amiable child, was named after his father's political hero, Timothy Pickering.[24] Hanson may not have known it at the time, but his wife was pregnant with another child, a boy.

Joining Hanson and his family for the horse ride to Baltimore was friend John Howard Payne. Knowing that their return was likely to cause a stir, Hanson emphasized discretion and told his friend not to acknowledge any of the other Federalist recruits they might encounter along the route in order to "avoid the imputation of entering the city with a guard."

Left: Hanson named his son after his political hero, Thomas Pickering, a U.S. senator from Massachusetts and fervent Federalist who was targeted by Republicans in Congress and later censured. On his return home to Massachusetts, Pickering met Hanson and later shared the news with his wife, writing of his encounter with "an interesting and able young man, named Alexander Contee Hanson." *Library of Congress*.

Below: The house at 45 Charles Street, described as "middling size" (see symbol), consisted of three floors, including an office and kitchen and entryway, with an additional back building. Poppleton Map. *Library of Congress*.

After dropping his wife and children at the home of a family member three miles outside the city for their safety, Hanson and Payne arrived in Baltimore. Their destination was 45 South Charles Street in Old Town, in the house rented by Jacob Wagner, the coeditor of the newspaper.

Wagner himself had already fled the city with his family and was in Georgetown making preparations for the new issue of the *Federal Republican*. Hanson's plan was to print the newspaper in Georgetown and then distribute it in Baltimore. To aid in this effort, he had assembled a "Spartan Band" of Federalists to help him defend the newspaper should the need arise. Reprisals were expected—and perhaps welcomed—but Hanson hoped that a show of force would dissuade the mob and permit civil authorities to assert control of the city and allow his newspaper to continue publishing.

ENTER "LIGHT-HORSE HARRY" LEE

The elder statesman of Hanson's band was General Henry Lee, better known as "Light-Horse Harry" Lee. A friend of Hanson's late father, Lee earned fame during the Revolutionary War while serving in George Washington's army and winning a surprise victory against the British in New Jersey with his adroit horsemanship. After the war, Lee had a successful political career, serving in the state assembly, winning election as governor of Virginia and later as a U.S. congressman. On top of his equestrian moniker, Lee was also well known for his eulogy at George Washington's funeral, in which he described the first president as "first in war, first in peace, and first in the hearts of his countrymen."

Lee's fortunes later took a turn for the worse after some ill-advised loans and land speculation, and the Revolutionary War hero ended up in debtors' prison in 1809. He worked on his memoirs while in jail and, after his release, settled in a modest home in Alexandria with his family, which included a young son named Robert E. Lee.

Lee arrived at 45 Charles Street in Baltimore on Sunday evening. As an ardent Federalist, he may have been motivated to help Hanson from his shared opposition to President Madison and the war, or perhaps it harkened the fifty-six-year-old general back to his earlier glory as a patriot and military hero, rather than his more recent notoriety as a debtor.

General Lee may have also found himself at the house merely by accident, as the mayor later claimed, reporting that the general told him he "came there by invitation to play a game of whist." That explanation seems improbable and was more likely a show of humor or defiance than anything else, though Lee did later tell a Massachusetts minister that he was not aware of Hanson's plan and was in Baltimore to make arrangements with a printer to publish his memoirs.[25]

For his part, Hanson admired Lee and knew the general's background would be invaluable to his effort. Hanson served as a lieutenant in the Maryland militia and was a crack shot, but he had never served in wartime

54

General "Light-Horse Harry" Lee was known as a brilliant military tactician during the Revolutionary War. Lee later learned about the dangers of the mob while governor of Virginia when he was sent to quell a brewing insurrection in western Pennsylvania over whiskey taxes. The incident, later known as the Whiskey Rebellion, taught Lee the perils of "sporting with public passions." *National Portrait Gallery, Smithsonian Institution.*

and was certainly no military leader. As a professional soldier, Lee was experienced in partisan warfare and brought the respect of a Revolutionary War hero whose career was closely linked to the late president Washington, father of the nation and an idolized figure. Hanson was also aware of another highlight in Lee's military career in which he helped defend a house from a regiment of British regulars with only ten men—just the kind of experience Hanson knew might come in handy in the days ahead.

Upon his arrival, Lee took command of the house and implemented a blueprint for its defense. In a lengthy letter to Hanson sent a week before his arrival in Baltimore, Lee outlined a series of tactical measures with specifics about how muskets, spare flints and cartridge shots should be placed and where personnel should be stationed room by room.[26] One recommendation involved collecting large stones and storing them in the cellar, then casting them from windows against any would-be assailants who tried to enter. Lee also reminded Hanson about the importance of feeding the troops: "Water and biscuit be sure to have in abundance."

Hanson worked out some of the arrangements in advance. While he and Payne traveled the countryside to recruit supporters, a young man identified as M'Clellan was sent ahead to secure a cache of weapons for the house on Charles Street, including twenty muskets. On Saturday afternoon, the day before Hanson's arrival, the next-door neighbor witnessed M'Clellan bringing in provisions by stagecoach, including three demijohns (large wicker-cased bottles) and later a heavy cloth-covered box. As instructed by Hanson, great efforts were made to conceal the weapons and avoid attracting attention, including marking a keg of powder as "Crackers."

Preparations continued in earnest throughout the day on Sunday as recruits arrived from the country. Some volunteers were tasked with preparing ammunition; others went to work reinforcing doors and barricading gates and windows. Visitors were instructed to make sure the door was kept locked and ensure that no weapons were visible through the windows. Still, the next-door neighbor reported hearing loud hammering noises.

GENERAL JAMES LINGAN ARRIVES

When Lee arrived, there were about a dozen men present in the house, including another Revolutionary War veteran, James McCubbin Lingan. General Lingan, then sixty-one years old, had spent a long stretch as a prisoner of war on board a British warship during the Revolution and, like Lee, was a respected military leader. Lingan and Lee were the senior statesmen, while the rest of the Federalist recruits were mainly contemporaries of Hanson's from Montgomery County and surrounding counties.

The men were loyal to Hanson and the Federalist cause, and many shared Hanson's view that they were engaged in a noble calling to defend the free press. In turning back the mob, they were upholding the same principles for which the Revolutionary War had been fought a generation before—and helping deliver Baltimore, and the nation, a necessary lesson in liberty over tyranny.

The older men who experienced the struggle for independence firsthand held the cause even dearer. On his way to Baltimore, General Lingan had stopped at the home of one young Federalist, Henry Gaither, and shared his own motivation. Gaither was about to head to church, and although he was Hanson's friend, he wasn't sure if he wanted to get involved. Lingan spoke powerfully of his own experience as a prisoner of war and what it meant to serve the cause of liberty and help establish a government where freedom of speech and freedom of the press are guaranteed.

The Baltimore mob threatened those "sacred privileges" Lingan told Gaither, and if they did not stand up to oppose such actions, "life itself was not worth possessing." The general's words must have had an impact, as the next day, Gaither left his home in Montgomery County and joined the Federalists at the house on Charles Street.

Gaither may not have been the only recruit to experience initial misgivings about the adventure upon which they were embarking. The prospect of an angry mob attacking them certainly sparked fears in the eyes of some of the young men. John Payne confided to Hanson his anxiety about how he might react to a first attack, "once the stones should first fly, the doors crash, and the glass shiver into atoms." Hanson tried to reassure his young friend, telling him any momentary fear was nothing compared to what might happen if city authorities failed to act to restrain the mob and violence ensued. His remarks could not have been soothing: Any bloodshed by the assailants, Hanson cautioned, and "the populace…would become exasperated and place us in a situation of unprecedented horror."

If Payne, the aspiring actor, was experiencing a case of stage fright, he still managed to keep his wits about him. He devised a clever plan to track the comings and goings of every man in the house to ensure there were always a minimum number of defenders by putting all their names on a slate.

While Payne and the others readied for their roles, General Lee and General Lingan took command, using their status as military leaders to impose order on Hanson's team and rein in excess zeal. Lee advised the group to be wary of a surprise attack and to make sure the lights were dimmed and noise kept to a minimum. The new edition of the newspaper was expected

Gaither would later name a son in honor of the general. William Lingan Gaither (portrait circa 1835) was born the following year. *Maryland State Archives.*

to arrive from Georgetown on Monday morning and all expected trouble, but both generals preached restraint and emphasized the importance of not taking any offensive action should the mob come calling.

The sun set just after seven o'clock on Sunday, July 26, and as darkness slowly descended on Baltimore, Hanson's team made final preparations. Last-minute measures that evening included blocking a passageway from Charles Street into the yard of the house and establishing a night watch rotation, which included Crabb, Gaither, Kilgour and Payne. With preparations in place and the new edition of the *Federal Republican* en route, Hanson went upstairs to retire for the night.

Around the corner at Gadsby's Tavern at the corner of Hanover and Baltimore Streets, the regulars were hanging out, probably hoisting plentiful pints of porter and ale. Members of the local Republican Party often gathered at Gadsby's for ward meetings and social occasions, and the First Baltimore Troop, a local militia group, had recently reformed and met there as well. The troop had invited "patriotic citizens" to join and pledged to patrol the streets to "suppress riots and mobs of the city."

In other words, there could hardly be a less receptive crowd for Hanson and his Federalist friends—except perhaps at Pamphilion's Hotel across town in Fell's Point, where a similar tavern scene was likely playing out. The patrons at Pamphilion's and Gadsby's may have been unaware of Hanson's return to Baltimore that evening, but word was already spreading in other parts of the city, despite the Federalists' attempts to keep a low profile.

A local cabinetmaker named Peter White, who lived nearby on Pratt Street, learned of Hanson's return around sundown. His mother, Jane, a widow, owned the Charles Street dwelling that Hanson and his team now occupied. White feared that the newspaper editor's return would invite an attack and lead to the destruction of his mother's property, so he decided to pay a visit that night.

It was between ten o'clock and eleven o'clock in the evening when White came calling. He was met at the door by two of the Federalists, who then alerted a resting Hanson. White wanted to know if the newspaper was to be published from the house and asked for assurances that his mother would be reimbursed for any damage, but Hanson demurred. He was counting on the fact that the mob might be more reluctant to attack if they knew the widow would suffer the property damage. White left unsatisfied, and Hanson, fatigued from riding all day, retired upstairs for the night. It was to be his last peaceful moment for some time.

THE FEDERALISTS STRIKE BACK

*A Mobocracy...Five weeks have elapsed since the suspension of this journal....
The outrages of the Mob, implicitly sanctioned if not originated by the highest
authorities in the country, are resolvable into a single point—a daring and
desperate attempt to intimidate and overawe the minority, to destroy the freedom of
speech and of the press.*
—Federal Republican, *July 27, 1812*

B ALTIMORE, JULY 27, 1812—The thud of the newspaper delivery at nine o'clock Monday morning was literal and figurative. Blazoned across five columns of the newly revived *Federal Republican* ran a caustic editorial, "A Mobocracy." What followed was Hanson's pointed critique of the city's response to the initial mob attack, with particular blame laid at the feet of Mayor Edward Johnson.

The mayor's failure to restore order empowered the mob to quash the liberty of speech and extinguish freedom of the press in the city, Hanson charged, much like French revolutionaries he so despised. Congress, Maryland's governor, the "ruffians" from Fell's Point and that "paltry French apothecary" also shared in the blame, but Hanson clearly put Mayor Johnson in his crosshairs. The civil authority had failed its most basic mission and, in a zealous march to war, had trampled on the very principles of liberty it espoused, he wrote: "They destroy Republicanism under the mask of supporting it, and violate the laws under the pretext of enforcing them."

On Monday morning (a "very fine pleasant day"), even before the new edition could be distributed around the city, another set of visitors arrived at the house on Charles Street to confront Hanson. Peter White returned with his mother, Jane White, the landlady, as soon as they had finished breakfast. The Whites were admitted and greeted by Hanson's assistant.

Mrs. White said she'd heard reports there was a printing press set up in the house and reminded him the house had not been rented for that purpose. She threatened to have the press taken down if that was the case. The Federalists were not in a cooperative mood and apparently did not share the fact that this latest newspaper had actually been printed in Georgetown and delivered to the city by express rider.

"About this time I became warm and a little irritated, for I believed an attack would be made on the house if Mr. Hanson remained in it," White recalled. He explained that his mother had reduced the regular rental fee from $400 a year to $350 per year based on assurances from Mrs. Wagner that she could take care of the property. Now he felt duped. The apparent intention to install a printing press only added insult to injury.

"I then proposed to pay them the money in question, if they would leave the house immediately," White said.

Hanson's "Spartan Band" grew throughout the day as news spread of his return to Baltimore. *Maryland Historical Society.*

Hanson joined in the conversation and adopted a more diplomatic approach. He assured Mrs. White that he would cover any repairs to the property, going so far as to offer to pay double the cost of whatever damage might be sustained. Hanson even agreed to show Peter White upstairs so he could see for himself what they were doing, but another Federalist objected to this, calling it "improper."

Frustrated again, Peter White and his mother left the house determined to seek redress elsewhere. As they were leaving, White's brother-in-law, Dennis Nowland, who had just learned of Hanson's return himself, caught up with the pair at the door, and all three marched off to find the mayor.

In the meantime, word of the new edition was spreading around the city. Around midmorning, William Barney, a prominent local merchant and son of naval hero Joshua Barney, stopped by the bookstore on Baltimore Street near Gadsby's Tavern. Stacked with the Bibles, encyclopedias, poetry books, magazines, stationery papers and bound *Don Quixote* volumes was the new edition of the *Federal Republican*.[27] Barney read the editorial, in particular the attack on Mayor Johnson, and had a visceral reaction.

"I observed, that it was libel," Barney said to the bookseller, who was known to be friendly with Hanson. The bookseller also knew something of Hanson's determination and advised Barney, a major in the militia, to seek his redress by lawful means. Hanson intended to resume publishing the newspaper in the city from the house on Charles Street, the bookseller told Major Barney, and warned him that "some of the most determined men in the United States were armed, and would re-establish [the newspaper] at every hazard."

Barney was nonplussed. "I gave as my opinion, that if blood was spilt by the persons he spoke of, the people of Baltimore would tear them to pieces," he replied and called Hanson's attempt to relaunch his newspaper "ridiculous."

Barney made a point to add that while the newspaper may have included "infamous pieces," he did not hear of any actual threats issued during his travels that day, and he himself did not believe an attack would be attempted. In fact, Barney later shared a laugh with Hanson's neighbors over the fuss the Federalists were making inside the house and how they would be "confoundedly disappointed" if no attack was actually forthcoming.

The day's events did not take long to reach the desk of Mayor Johnson. He had been out of the city, probably at his residence in the country. He returned with his wife to bring their son to the family doctor when he learned of Hanson's return.

The mayor's office was located in Old Town in the rear of an insurance building. Across the street, a garment shop advertised the latest in female fashions, including riding hats and pelisses—fur-trimmed ladies' jackets then in style. When he arrived at this office, the mayor found Peter White, Jane White and her son-in-law Dennis Nowland all waiting for him.

Nowland introduced his mother-in-law to the mayor and explained the situation with her rented dwelling house that Hanson and his cohorts now occupied and refused to relinquish. Mrs. White "dreaded the safety of her house in consequence of the reported threats of the populace of the city," he told the mayor, and asked him to intervene before any damage could occur.

The mayor was noncommittal. "If they are legally in possession of your property, under a lease, you cannot dispossess them," he said. As to the rumor that Hanson had printed his newspaper in the house, or intended to set up a printing press, the mayor recommended they to speak to an attorney. "Your remedy is an action of damages for violation of the contract."

Nowland pressed their case, asking if the mayor would call for help from civil or military authorities if needed. White pointed out that a mob had already attacked the first office Hanson occupied so there was ample reason to worry. The mayor stressed the need to follow the law and advised that any trespassers would be brought to justice. He later recalled the back-and-forth conversation in a deposition:

"Can you defend the property?" Nowland asked.

"I have no doubt of it," the mayor replied.

"Will you defend my property?" Nowland asked.

"As soon as the property of any man in the city," the mayor said.

"If you will permit me to arm myself, and some of my friends, I can easily turn them out, and take possession of the house," Nowland said.

"You have no right to do so, and if you resort to violence, do not call on me for assistance, you shall have none from me," the mayor warned, "if you use arms, arms will be used against you, and I never will put myself between two fires."

The mayor stressed that he did not wish to get in the middle of an armed conflict, telling Nowland he "would not place himself in a situation to be shot at."

Mayor Johnson may have been intentionally downplaying the likelihood of violence to avoid potential bloodshed or just to placate angry constituents. In either case, he ushered the group out of his office, citing a meeting with the city commissioners, and offered Mrs. White some parting advice. "Madam, you need not be under any apprehension, for I do not think the property will be injured." He urged them to report the names of anyone who made specific threats against the property so he could have them arrested. Nowland and the Whites left the mayor's office, heading back toward Charles Street. They were not yet ready to give up.

UNREST IN FELL'S POINT

By midday, Baltimore buzzed with news of Hanson's return. In the salty seafaring neighborhood of Fell's Point, the new edition of the *Federal Republican* was the topic of conversation for men at the local coffeehouse, including James Biays, a popular figure who served as Republican ward leader and militia officer and had a history of run-ins and ties with mobs.[28] One of the men called Hanson's return an "imprudent act" and predicted it would trigger another riot. Such talk was not uncommon, especially around Fell's Point, which welcomed all manner of schooner and cargo to its port but did not take kindly to Federalist interlopers or British sympathizers.

Even before the first newspaper riot, complaints about Hanson's publication were common at the gritty taverns, hotels and coffeehouses that dotted the boot-shaped district. "Respectable people" in the neighborhood felt the newspaper was "so obnoxious that the editors must either alter its tone, or it must be stopped," one resident recounted. Biays, a ship joiner who grew prosperous as a commodity trader, was a Presbyterian and an ardent Jeffersonian who had no love for Hanson.[29] The feeling was mutual, for Hanson frequently jabbed Fell's Point and once labeled Biays "a notorious coward and unprincipled bully."[30]

If Hanson had a more bitter foe in the city than James Biays, it was probably Thomas Wilson, editor of the *Baltimore Sun*, a staunchly Republican newspaper launched the prior year. Wilson was an excitable man who wielded influence in Republican circles with his sharp rhetoric. He had actively encouraged the demolition of Hanson's first newspaper office on Gay Street and made it known he did not think the publication should be allowed to return to Baltimore.

Wilson learned the news of Hanson's return from Dennis Nowland, who, after leaving the mayor's office earlier in the day, continued his crusade to protect his mother-in-law's property. He stopped in to see Wilson before heading to Fell's Point, and later detailed the encounter.

James Biays (*center on horse*) was a prominent resident of Fell's Point, a hotbed of anti-Federalist sentiment. Biays is depicted here during the Battle of North Point. *From* The Pictorial Field-Book of the War of 1812.

"Mr. Wilson, have you heard the news this morning?" Nowland asked.

"Yes—Nathan Tyson is loading a vessel with flour for the British troops in Spain, and it is doubtful whether she will be permitted to go," the editor replied.

"No, that is not the news, but that the *Federal Republican* paper was circulating through the city."

Nowland explained his fears that the mob would come after Hanson and destroy his mother-in-law's property. Knowing that the editor carried influence with the mob's ringleaders, he asked him to intervene on his behalf. Wilson told Nowland he would do what he could to preserve Mrs. White's property but felt certain that an attack was unavoidable.

"People had become so incensed against the paper that they would not suffer it to be again established in that place, and abuse the government as they had done," Wilson warned.

FORTIFYING THE CHARLES STREET HOUSE

Back at Charles Street, Hanson's "Spartan Band" was growing. His original recruits, most hailing from Montgomery County, were augmented by Federalists in Baltimore sympathetic to the cause. Some visitors came just to wish Hanson well on the revival of the newspaper, while others stuck around for the confrontation they all expected later. Per orders of Generals Lee and Lingan, the men continued to keep the front door locked and avoid any unnecessary display of weapons.

Whether curiosity seekers, Federalist supporters or Republican emissaries, visitors flowed in and out of the three-story house at 45 Charles Street throughout the afternoon. Many later attested to the defensive mindset of those present. Hanson, Lingan and Lee all expected reprisals, but they meant no injury to others and intended to act solely on the defensive if the mob attacked, one visitor reported.

"I went into almost all, perhaps all the rooms in the house, to observe in what state of defence it was—and in several of the rooms saw some muskets, and if I mistake not some swords—how many I cannot say. There were also one or two pair of pistols on the table in the room below stairs, and a servant was employed in the kitchen cutting slugs," the visitor said. "Although I had reason to believe that a great portion of the people of Baltimore were hostile to the re-establishment of the paper—yet I did not believe they would attack the office when they discovered that it was prepared for defence."

Hanson continued to express outward optimism about his plan whether he really felt it or not. He encountered Peter White again later in the day and offered reassurances to allay his mother's fears; this was not the first time he'd been threatened by a mob and he could handle himself. Hanson told White that his mother should not worry about all the talk; the mob could do little more than break windows.

His sentiments were largely shared by Mayor Johnson. Despite being the primary target of Hanson's editorials, Johnson displayed a thick skin. Referring to the new edition of the *Federal Republican*, he remarked there was "nothing in it that could excite the public indignation or feelings." Other than a routine meeting with his commissioners, there's no evidence the mayor took any affirmative action on Monday to address Hanson's return. For a mayor whose political radar was usually finely tuned, this outlook was surprising to many. Johnson may have been more preoccupied with his sick child and getting back to his country house later that afternoon.

He left the office sometime before three o'clock and headed back to his home on King George Street to tend to his family. On the way, he likely passed by the corner medicine shop, Warner and Hanna, which advertised cures like "Dr. Robertson's Infallible Worm Destroying Losenges" and "Dr. Dyotts Anti-Bilious Pills." Thrice daily doses of the latter promised to cure symptoms of yellow fever, chronic pain, indigestion, gout, rheumatism and even flatulence.[31]

After an early supper, Johnson planned to join his family for a ride back to the countryside around four o'clock. His bags were packed, and the carriage was parked at the door, ready to depart, when he received a visit from John Hargrove, the city register.

Hargrove, a Republican, shared an office with the mayor and also served as pastor at the New Jerusalem Church. He came calling to relay a message from a militia officer who'd come to the office after the mayor had left. The man believed an attack on Hanson's building was imminent and urged the mayor to call out the civil authorities right away. Displaying the leisurely haste of a practiced bureaucrat, Hargrove first advised the man to tell the mayor himself—then agreed to relay the message, but only after he'd closed the office and had his supper. Hargrove was true to this word and recounted his conversation to the mayor after his repast.

"Did he assign any reasons for his fears?" the mayor asked after hearing the story.

"He had reasons," Hargrove said with evident skepticism.

The mayor was not convinced. "I do not think, Mr. Hargrove, there will be any such attack as [he] fears."

The city register concurred with the mayor and predicted that "nothing disagreeable would take place."

With the late afternoon sun dipping in the sky, Mayor Johnson mounted the carriage and rode out of the city with his family. Any worries of the mob, the *Federal Republican* or Alexander Hanson were left in his wake.

RETURN OF THE MOB

I will lead you on, and we will kill every damn'd rascal in the house.

MONDAY EVENING—The sun was setting in Old Town, and all remained quiet at 45 Charles Street. General Lee returned to the house around seven o'clock. More reinforcements had arrived earlier in the evening, and there were by then upward of twenty-five men garrisoned inside, most armed with muskets, bayonets, pistols and swords. Lee reminded them to keep the noise and candlelight to a minimum to avoid attracting attention.

Spirits ran high, and the men spoke of their sense of duty. The conversation eventually turned to the topic on everyone's mind. Would the Baltimore mob return to pay them a visit that evening? The general consensus was no. General Lee certainly expected trouble later in the week but expressed confidence that the house was amply defended and felt they would be safe at least for this evening. He even sent home three men who rode in from Montgomery County so that they could find sleeping quarters.

"We were satisfied that no attack was meditated that night," John Howard Payne recalled.

Hanson was less confident. He dispatched one man to secure more muskets and asked Payne to take a ride over to Fell's Point to scout the neighborhood. Rumors abounded, and Hanson wanted to know what the "sons of the disloyal and turbulent" were up to that evening. So Payne and another volunteer saddled their horses and rode through Old Town, crossing over the Jones Falls to Fell's Point. After a lengthy patrol, the pair determined that "everything was tranquil" and began the journey back to the house to report on their mission.

Not everything remained tranquil on Charles Street.

No sooner had Payne left than a stagecoach drove up in front of the Federalist house and stopped by the door to drop off supplies. Watching the scene with curiosity was a small gang of boys who had gathered nearby, likely with mischievous intent. The boys, "of various sizes, in number twelve or fifteen," jumped back as several men emerged from the coach with swords drawn and then they watched as the men unloaded weapons and ammunition and delivered them into the Federalists' three-story brick house. The muskets made a rattling sound according to a neighbor.

Hanson and his cohorts made final arrangements on Sunday and Monday to fortify the Charles Street house and prepare for any mob retaliation. *Library of Congress.*

The boys, too, may have been rattled, but their bravado quickly returned. "The Tories are collecting muskets to kill the Republicans," the boys were heard to say. As soon as the stagecoach drove off, they began by hurling threats and insults toward the house and then progressed to bricks and paving stones, egged on by several men standing in the street. The loud noises and shouts attracted more attention, and the passel of boys quickly grew.

By eight o'clock, "a herd of Irishmen and negroes and Frenchmen, and ragamuffins, had congregated and … commenced a most violent attack upon the house." Cries of "damned Tories, traitors and rebels" were shouted along with threats to breach the house and kill those inside. The men pelted the walls, windows and front door with a volley of cobblestones, breaking glass and destroying the shutters. "The crash of shivered glass, falling on all sides…was tremendous," Hanson recalled.[32]

Inside the house, the Federalists debated their next move. General Lee made it clear that no one was to fire without approval and unless compelled to in order to save lives. Lee knew he was dealing with a contingent of headstrong young men, and he was determined to maintain order, even in the face of hostile forces. He assigned each man defensive roles, putting Hanson in charge of the second floor while James P. Heath was tasked with protecting the first floor. Heath moved the lights to the back of the room and posted men near the front foyer to defend the entryway in case the door was forced open. He had about ten "stout" men helping him, and Hanson had about a dozen on the second floor. Five men were posted in the back of the house to defend against a rear attack, and a remaining force was stationed on the third floor under the command of Hanson's brother-in-law.

From his vantage upstairs, Hanson opened the window shutters and called out to the rioters gathering outside. This house was his "castle," Hanson warned; he and his men had a lawful right to occupy and defend it, and if the mob did not stand down, he would be compelled to fire on them. The words of warning, and several subsequent attempts, did little to deter the mob, and they resumed their barrage of brickbats. "Tear the damned Tory out of his castle—break open the door," the mob was heard to exclaim.

The words of Dennis Nowland were equally ineffective. Nowland arrived on the scene not long after the first group of boys began throwing stones and—as he'd feared all day— found his mother-in-law's house getting the brunt of the abuse. He vainly tried to dissuade the rioters, explaining that they were damaging the property of an innocent widow—but they were having none of it.

"No, Hanson, the damn'd Tory, is our object, and we will have him," one man replied.

If being Hanson's unwitting ally wasn't bad enough, Nowland's luck soon turned from bad to worse. In response to the barrage of stones hurled at the house, one of the Federalists retaliated by throwing a stove plate from the upper story. The metal plate fell to the pavement below and right onto his foot. Nowland hollered in pain as the force of the plate amputated several of his toes. He could no longer walk and had to be carried home.

While the battle brewed outside Charles Street, seeds of contention were growing inside the house, primarily between General Lee and Hanson. Lee counseled a conservative course: play defense and wait for city officials to intervene. After news of this latest disturbance reached the civil authority, surely they would act decisively to suppress further rioting, he reasoned. The brash young Hanson had less patience. He wanted to return fire and engage the mob. He urged Lee to look at the now shattered windows as evidence of the mob's intent.

"We must not mind our windows," Lee replied, according to one witness. "They are in the wrong. We must be sure to keep them in the wrong; they will get ashamed of their own conduct, and go away."

A middle course was adopted. The Federalists fired a warning shot from the upper floor over the heads of the mob. The tactic may have briefly intimidated the crowd, but the effect was temporary and the rioters soon renewed their attacks with greater intensity once they realized there was no real danger.

"Fire, Fire, you damned Tories! Fire! We are not afraid of you," one rioter yelled. Before a growing audience of bystanders, the men pressed forward and continued their assault. The windows were "beaten to pieces," and shattered glass littered the floors.

Inside, Heath pushed chairs, tables and furniture forward to help barricade the entry and front door, and upstairs, the men readied heavy logs of wood, which they could roll out the windows onto the crowd if necessary. One man had his pistol knocked from his hands by a rock and several received blows, but General Lee continued to insist the men hold their fire. Unless the assailants entered the house, they were not to retaliate, he ordered, knowing the Federalists would be judged harshly for any bloodshed by rioters, unless it was a defensive act. The decision was not necessarily a popular one with the majority of men in the house, which Lee acknowledged.

"Indignant at the revilings and vulgar abuse with which the mob continued to bespatter them and conscious of their legal right to kill all who assaulted the house they were very anxious to use their arms," Lee recalled. The young men were not keen to accept the "stern mandate of their leader who forbade their fire."

General Lee's gravitas as a Revolutionary War hero held sway, and his men, though civilians, followed the command of their military leader and mostly held their musket fire. Several bystanders remarked on the "extraordinary forbearance" displayed by the men inside in the house in face of such a belligerent crowd.

For unknown reasons, a man named Rufus Bigelow decided forbearance was not his forte and elected to leave the house. By this time, it was between nine o'clock and ten o'clock at night. Bigelow was a local merchant from the city and must have borne some resemblance to Jacob Wagner (now safely ensconced in Georgetown), for when Bigelow made his escape, he was spotted by the mob and mistaken for Wagner.

"There is Wagner, kill the damn'd Tory!" they cried.

Bigelow was knocked down and pummeled with fists and sticks. Badly injured, he was carried away and brought around the corner to an assembly hall known as Mallet's Dancing Hall, where a crowd gathered, attracted by the spectacle.

By this time, John Howard Payne was returning from his Fell's Point reconnaissance ride. He saw the commotion outside the dancing hall and quickly surmised what had occurred in his absence. Payne spotted one of the mob's ringleaders standing next to a large tree and listened to him rallying the crowd. "That ball was aimed at me—the Tories ought to be hang'd upon this tree," the man exhorted, and succeeded in raising the mob's fury. Realizing he would not be able to rejoin his friends back inside the house, Payne headed off to find help.

Some time after ten o'clock, he paid a frantic call to the home of William Gwynn, an attorney and prominent local Federalist, waking him from his sleep. After hearing the account of the mob attacks, Gwynn dressed and accompanied an anxious Payne back to Charles Street. They observed the chaotic scene in front of Hanson's house and decided it would not be safe to enter, so instead the pair walked farther up Charles Street to the home of Brigadier General John Stricker, a successful merchant and prominent Republican who served as commander of the city militia.

ENTER JOHN STRICKER

Described as a handsome man, Stricker, age fifty-three, was of Swiss descent with dark hair and graying sideburns. He had served in battle during the Revolutionary War and was later called out to help put down the Whiskey Rebellion but had thus far expressed great reluctance to inject himself into the violent fracas unfolding a few houses down the road. Earlier in the evening, the general was visited by an impatient Peter White, who requested help to protect his mother's property and disperse the growing mob gathered in front of her house.

Stricker did not adopt a very a sympathetic tone. "I do not disperse mobs," he reportedly told White in a "contemptuous" manner and then advised that White's mother should have known better than to rent property to someone like Alexander Hanson. A frustrated White soon left Stricker's house and returned home.

White was not the only one to seek the general's assistance. Even before the arrival of Payne and Gwynn, several residents came calling to ask him to order out the militia. General Stricker steadfastly maintained that he did not have the authority to do so without an official request from the civil authority, and Mayor Johnson had left the city earlier in the day and

Brigadier General John Stricker lived on Charles Street, a short distance from the Federalists' house. *Maryland Historical Society*.

was out in the countryside, blissfully unaware of the subsequent drama. Stricker commanded the Baltimore Brigade but also served as a Republican political appointee and, like the mayor, was not eager to protect a band of miscreant Federalists.

In this case, Stricker's cautious approach was both legally accurate and political advantageous. Maryland state law, just amended in January, called for two justices of the peace to sign off before allowing a commanding officer to order out the militia. Stricker knew that if he mustered the troops there was likely to be bloodshed, so his strict adherence to the letter of the law provided some convenient political cover. He had also learned his lesson from a past incident in which he faced recriminations for ordering out the militia without proper authority.

Still, with the repeated calls from citizens for assistance, the throngs of rioters passing by his house and the ominous sounds of drumbeats and musket fire punctuating the air, Stricker realized he could not sit idly on his hands. He made it be known he would issue the order if the appropriate process was followed.

The order was promptly drafted, and after William Gwynn, the Federalist attorney, made some minor edits, it was ready to be signed. Enter the bureaucracy. A debate broke out among Stricker's legal advisors whether a justice of the peace was required or if a civil magistrate could sign the order. One justice of the peace promptly agreed to sign, but getting the second signature proved elusive. Several magistrates lived nearby and some had even been at Stricker's home that evening, but when it came time to ink the decisive signature most demurred, declined or disappeared.

While the bureaucracy puttered, Hanson and his Federalist cohorts remained barricaded in the house, trapped by a growing swarm of rioters. Hanson could see that the situation was growing untenable. "The moment was critical. If the mob were permitted to enter the house it was manifest that we must kill them or be slain ourselves. If we had attempted to escape we most certainly would have been massacred, unless we had first dispersed the mob by firing on, and killing some of them. On whatever side, therefore, we turned no alternative appeared but to fire on the assailants or be slaughtered by them," Hanson wrote.[33]

Dr. Gale Leads the Charge

The ringleader egging on the crowd of rioters was an enigmatic Frenchman named Dr. Thaddeus Gale, who touted the curative practice of "medical electricity" and probably arrived in Baltimore only lately. Described as "lank and pale,"[34] Dr. Gale was at least fifty years old and had started his career as an itinerant physician in New York and New England soon after the American Revolution. He held strong views on politics and medicine and wrote a radical book advocating a form of shock therapy. Like the French apothecary who led the first mob attack in June, Dr. Gale was viewed as a violent man—and something of a quack. One poet colorfully described him as a "lurking villain" and "a vendor of nostrums."[35]

Multiple witnesses on the scene attested to Dr. Gale's maniacal ways, calling him "excessively noisy and turbulent" and the "most riotous and leading assassins among them."

Earlier in the night, he had incited the boys gathered outside the house to throw stones and later was spotted striking Rufus Bigelow with a stick. A rousing speech outside the dance hall had ginned up the rioters further, and he now called for a direct frontal assault.

"I will lead you on, and we will kill every damn'd rascal in the house," he shouted.

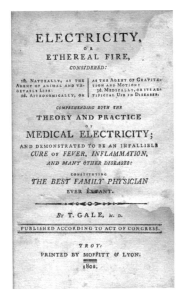

Dr. Gale's book *Electricity, or Ethereal Fire* was published in 1802 and is considered one of the first known treatises on electrotherapy. Gale maintained that the medical use of electricity could treat all manner of illness ranging from headaches and hemorrhoids to epilepsy and "madness." In his frequent advertisements in local newspapers, Gale claimed the title of "the best Family Physician ever extant" but his medical career was largely an obscure one—at least during his lifetime. History has been more kind, and Gale's book has been cited in medical journals for his work using electricity as medicine. *Google Books.*

Dr. Gale advanced toward the Federalist front door accompanied by a cadence of beating drums and a contingent of rioters on his heels. The door was already damaged from the cobblestone barrage, and he easily forced it open. The enraged doctor pushed forward and prepared to make good on his deadly threats as he crossed the threshold and stepped into the foyer. The scene was later described in a poem:

> *Him faction singled in the lawless fray,*
> *A daring game with desperate hand to play;*
> *With fury flashing from his haggard eye,*
> *He struck the door—the mob exulting cry—*[36]

For General Lee, this was a step too far. He had successfully kept his impatient band of men in check, but now the rioters had breached the house itself. Standing in the front parlor, Lee spoke to Dr. Gale in a calm, measured voice. "I assure you, sir, you have now entered that door as far as you can come this night," he warned.

The next sound was gunfire. A lead ball fired from inside the house struck Gale, and he fell backward onto the pavement. Several other shots were fired from the window and staircase, and a brief volley ensued. The musket fire startled the rioters, who were growing accustomed to the Federalists' practiced pacifism, but they quickly responded.

The return fire wounded one of the Federalists, Ephraim Gaither, who had thrown out the metal stove earlier in the evening. Gaither was stationed on the third floor and may have been shot by a man standing behind a poplar tree a few feet from the house. The front door remained open, and a Federalist voice was heard to call out, "Clear the door," followed by another musket shot from within that wounded a local baker standing on the street.

A short distance away on Lexington Street, a sharp knock on the door roused Major Barney from his sleep. It was around eleven o'clock in the evening, and Barney had gone to bed several hours earlier thinking all would be quiet that evening. He raised the window, and in the bright moonlight, he saw in the street one of Stricker's men who quickly apprised him of the night's tumultuous events. After dressing in his military uniform, Major Barney rode his horse over to General Stricker's house, where the search was still on for a second signature. Several men had been dispatched to locate another justice of the peace, but so far efforts had been unsuccessful. In the meantime, Stricker asked Major Barney to round up as many horsemen as he could and return, by which time he hoped to have finalized the muster order.

Back at Charles Street, the brief exchange of gunfire had ended, but the body of Dr. Gale remained prone on the pavement. The musket shot proved a fatal blow. As the rioters realized their leader was killed, the beating drum stopped. His body was promptly retrieved, and the group of rioters carried him off as they retreated from the house in different directions.

The death of their de facto leader, Dr. Gale, one of the first fatalities of the evening, served to enrage the mob even further, and soon a call came out to find a cannon. A local carter named Jones volunteered, and he called for several men to join him: "Follow me, I wilt shew you where to get a cannon."

ATTEMPTS AT DIPLOMACY

Andrew Boyd watched the scene escalate with growing alarm. During the first newspaper attack in June, Boyd, a respected Republican resident, had interceded at the bank to help dispel the mob and saw his opportunity to do so again. "I immediately called to the people to come away, and not expose themselves to be shot," Boyd recounted, "[and] asked if something could not be done to stop the effusion of blood."

After a brief discussion with the rioters, Boyd agreed to go inside the house and present their demands to Hanson directly. The attempt at diplomacy was admirable but doomed to fail. The mob proposed that Hanson and his men give themselves up, a capitulation Boyd knew they would never agree to. He went anyway, and as expected, Hanson rejected the idea out of hand, though he did offer one concession: if the mob agreed to stop their attacks and safeguard his men, he would agree to stop publishing the newspaper from Baltimore.

If true, it was a remarkable concession for a man whose mission was founded on a core belief of defending the liberty of the press at all costs. Hanson may have been attempting to defuse the situation and protect his men, or perhaps had some ulterior motive, but it would not matter. The mob, after hearing of Hanson's refusal to surrender on their specified terms, had little interest in hearing anything further and certainly brooked no foolish talk of compromise. They shouted down Boyd, the loyal Republican, and showered him with abuse, including cries of "Tory."

The mob was indeed a fickle foe. But Boyd was luckier than Samuel Hoffman, another of Hanson's young Federalist recruits who had been garrisoned inside the house. For whatever reason, Hoffman decided he'd had enough and, after Boyd's visit, made a break for the front door. He didn't get far. As he exited the house and crossed Charles Street, Hoffman was knocked down by rioters and repeatedly beaten. He tried to rise from the ground and was struck down again. Finally, a group of rioters carried him off to the watch house, stating their intentions to hang him. He was later found lying there on a bench, "weltering in his blood, and much disfigured."

Patience was wearing thin everywhere. Major Barney returned to General Stricker's house to report back and check on his orders. He had limited success raising the cavalry; many of his men could not be located, and some would not report—including even his trumpeter. When Major Barney left again to check on them, fewer than thirty men had assembled at the muster point on the corner of Market Street. "I was mortified, and expressed it, that I should hold a command of men who, when it came to a push, would not turn out," the major told Stricker.

Still, he made clear to those men who did report that theirs was a defensive mission. "You will not draw your swords unless particularly ordered by me, and when that order is given, I hope you will use them like men," Barney commanded his troop. He further warned them not to be thin-skinned: "You are to put up with every insult that tongue can utter."

A few blocks away, the crowd outside 45 Charles Street had swelled to more than five hundred, though determining who was actively engaged in the rioting and who was merely gawking was nearly impossible in the swarming mass. While the rioters at the first newspaper attack in June had represented a broad mix of Baltimore's middle and lower classes—including master craftsmen, shopkeepers and property owners—the composition this evening had now shifted more toward the lower rungs of the economic ladder.[37] The slain mob leader, Dr. Gale, was clearly an educated (if eccentric) man, but his disciples by and large were not. The men continued to hurl rocks at the house and revel in the fray with loud huzzas, drumbeats and occasional musket fire while they anticipated the arrival of a cannon. Hanson was taunted with chants and insults, called a "damned Tory" and "a British hireling." The crowd even poked fun at his diminutive size with cries for "'Little Ellick' to show his eyes out the window."[38]

Realizing the walls might soon be closing in on them, General Lee decided to send one of his Federalist lieutenants out on a flanking maneuver. He ordered James Heath to covertly exit the house and seek out a handful of additional Federalist sympathizers who were "friendly to the empire of laws." Heath was directed to arm the men with muskets and find a concealed perch behind the mob's front line such that they might fire from

The First German Reformed Church (*background*) with its two-hundred-foot-tall spire and town clock was a prominent feature of the city skyline until it was torn down in the latter half of the nineteenth century. *Library of Congress.*

the rear in the event the rioters pressed forward with a coordinated attack. Heath was eager to help, and with two or three additional men, he left the house through the back door. They did not get far. After scaling the brick wall and landing on the other side, the Federalists were immediately met by a contingent of rioters.

"I was surrounded and cut off from the house," Heath recalled. "I received a blow on my left shoulder, which had very near brought me to the ground, but I recovered, and drew from my bosom a dirk, which I struck with in different directions," he said. Heath managed to get lost in the crowd, but his mission was clearly a bust and he was now cut off from his fellow Federalists inside the house.

Towering nearly two hundred feet above the bedlam stood the handsome spire of the German Reformed Church with its landmark town clock. The metal hands aligned at midnight, signaling the close of a remarkable day in the city's history. The once peaceful streets of Baltimore were now stained with blood, but for Hanson and his Federalist band, the worst was yet to come.

7

CAVALRY TO THE RESCUE?

*No murderer shall escape with my knowledge,
and that I pledge you my word as a man and a soldier.*

TUESDAY EARLY MORNING—Alexander Hanson and his fellow Federalists watched in darkness through the windows as the cavalry finally arrived. It was near two o'clock in the morning, and the crowd of rioters on Charles Street thinned to thirty or forty men. A decisive show of force and flash of iron might well end the standoff, they reasoned.

The initial response from the mob was promising. At the first sound of horses trampling afoot, many fled with cries of "the troop is coming, the troop is coming," but their fear was fleeting. Major William Barney, mindful that only a fraction of his cavalry had mustered, decided he must rely on the powers of persuasion more than force, and once the defensive posture of the cavalry was known, the rioters reemerged. Barney dismounted his horse and addressed a group of rioters congregated in a nearby alley, invoking his family name to remind the men he was one of them. He had earlier removed the feather from his cap and took off his Society of the Cincinnati eagle ribbon so as to avoid any class divisions or being mistaken for a foreigner.

"My name is Barney, and when you know that, you need not enquire into my politics, they are the same as yours. I am sent to preserve the peace of the city, and by God I will do it; and now my friends disperse and go home," he told them.

Though he occupied the opposing side of the political spectrum, William Bedford Barney's worldview was influenced much like Hanson's. As a young boy of about thirteen, Barney once joined his father on board a ship sailing from Baltimore to France. Young William was much taken with his time in Paris and developed a strong admiration of the French, his father later wrote.[39]

Those youthful impressions still informed his views. Now thirty years old and recently promoted to major in the militia, Barney was a dedicated Republican and staunch supporter of this new war against England, but the rioters were still skeptical of his intent.

"Are you come to take the Tory murderers prisoners?" they asked.

"No! I have no authority," Barney replied.

"Are you come to protect them?" they asked.

"I am come to protect them as well as you, and to protect you as well as them," the major assured the group.

"Do you mean to let the murderers escape?" the rioters asked.

"No murderer shall escape with my knowledge, and that I pledge you my word as a man and a soldier," Barney said and pulled out the paper showing his orders from General Stricker. He received three loud cheers in response. He may have earned the confidence of some in the mob, but he could not prevail upon them to stand down. Still, his attempts at rapprochement would pay off later.

After his conversation with the mob members, Barney walked over in front of the Charles Street house and stood until he was recognized. He had engaged with the Republicans—now it was time for the Federalists.

"Who comes there?" a voice was heard from inside the house.

"A friend," Major Barney replied.

"Who are you, and what's your business?" the unidentified Federalist asked.

"My name is Barney, and I come to protect persons and property," he replied.

"We are very glad to see you sir," came the reply. Barney was asked by what authority he acted upon, and he held up a copy of his orders from General Stricker.

Inside the house, Hanson and others remained skeptical of Barney's motives. They had watched him dismount and converse with the mob, and while they could not hear the substance of the conversation, they heard the three cheers of approval from the crowd. His friendly and familiar tone with the rioters—General Lee referred to it as "soft and conciliating"—also raised warning bells. Some suspected that Barney intended to arrest the Federalists and bring them up on charges for the death of Dr. Gale and any

Joshua Barney (*pictured*), a decorated naval officer, served with distinction in the American Revolution and later in the War of 1812. His son, William Bedford Barney, was married to Anne Chase, daughter of Supreme Court Justice Samuel Chase. The younger Barney would need all of his diplomatic and military skills to hold back the Baltimore mob. *New York Public Library*.

other slain rioters. Lee, who had studiously attempted to avoid confrontation all night, was inclined to believe in the sincerity of Barney's words, while Hanson remained mistrustful.

When the Federalists pressed Barney about his intentions, the major reiterated his intent to protect the house and the "safety and honor" of those

Major Barney (4) and General Stricker (1) as later depicted at the Battle of North Point. *From* The Pictorial Field-Book of the War of 1812.

in it. His cordial tone with the mob was necessary to maintain their trust, he explained. The deception was only intended for the rioters, he said—a necessary ruse to keep them in check. His argument was certainly logical, if not fully convincing to the Federalists.

It was apparently sufficient for General Lee. He spoke to Major Barney through the window in the front room of the house. "Captain Barney—we are ready to surrender to the civil authority if the mob will disperse; we will surrender to you sir—but the mob must first disperse."

"I told him I had no authority to receive a surrender, but I would endeavor to get the mob to disperse," Barney replied. But when he consulted with the rioters, they were not in a bargaining mood. The men told the major they would disperse only after the "murderers" surrendered as prisoners.

This was too much even for General Lee. The Federalists would never march out as prisoners and be subject to "the insults and scoffs of the mob," he informed Barney. Better to stay and perish in the house, Lee said, sounding more like the young Hanson.

Barney was not ready to give up his attempt to broker a peaceful solution. He told Lee the mob was concerned that some of the Federalists would escape if they all dispersed. Might the Federalists be willing to write down a list of names of those in the house in order to satisfy the mob? he asked. Lee did not object to this request. The Federalists felt they were on the side of the righteous in defending the house and the free press and "had done nothing that they were afraid to answer for," he told Barney.

NEW WEAPON OF WAR

The standoff might have de-escalated at this point but for an untimely interruption. Major Barney's primary focus may have been the art of diplomacy, but some of the rioters were more interested in the theory of superior firepower. They had finally secured a cannon and were now in the process of moving it into position.

"Major Barney, they are now bringing the cannon down Uhler's alley, and will fire it in a minute if you don't make haste sir," Barney was told. He ran down the street to the alley and spotted a group of men with the cannon. The limber cart usually used to transport artillery was missing, so the men pulled it toward the scene with drag ropes.

"I told them I was a friend, and cried to them to halt," the major recounted. The words were ignored.

The men warned him to get out of the way and continued to drag the artillery piece down the alley toward the Federalists' house. Barney decided to take matters a step further and positioned his chest in front of the cannon with his hands on the muzzle. The rioters pressed forward and pushed him along with the cannon until they had reached Charles Street.

There they encountered another contingent of rioters, the same group with which Barney had conversed a short time earlier and had given him three cheers. The goodwill he earned paid off. "Hear Major Barney, hear him! Hear what he has got to say, hear Major Barney!" they rallied their fellow rioters.

Barney seized the opportunity. "I mounted the gun, repeated what I had before said to the mob, assured them there was no danger of anyone escaping, that I had pledged my word to that effect." If it became necessary to fire the cannon, he would give the order himself, he said. With that, Barney demanded that the lit match be handed over, and it was. He let the match drop to the ground, and it extinguished itself.

Still, the rioters were not ready to abandon their new weapon. Barney stood vigilant, ready to intercede again if they should attempt to light the powder. At one point, he asked the mob members to point the muzzle away from the house, but they refused.

Barney did succeed in convincing one of the mob's leaders, a local tailor named John B. Gill, to use his influence to prevent the cannon from being fired. Gill, who was also a militia member, agreed only after hearing assurances that city officials would soon return and take the Federalists into custody.

"Lads, this gun belongs to the artillery company I belong to, I am used to it, and can handle it better than you can," Gill proclaimed to his fellow rioters. "Give me charge of it, and when the Major here breaks his word, by God we'll give it to the Tories," he said.

Gill's participation and influence with the mob helped prevent an escalation of force but also reinforced the same worries Mayor Johnson expressed after the first newspaper attack. The mayor had dithered about whether to call out the militia, knowing their ranks were filled with the same kind of men prone to join the mob. The line between militia and rioter was blurry and Gill personified this dilemma.

The militia cavalry troops, which had lined up in a defensive position to the side of the Federalist house, moved rightward so as to be out of the direct firing line of the cannon. The men shifted on their own without orders from any of the militia officers, which angered Barney. "Damn'd them for moving," he said, knowing the fact that his horsemen stood in the blast range dissuaded the rioters from firing the cannon at the Federalist house. The inference was clear: the mob would not fire on its own.

The ranks of militia defending the house could have been larger but for the reluctance to even call out some of the city's troops. One of Major Barney's officers who commanded a squadron of light cavalry from Fell's Point voiced concerned about what might happen if he tried to muster his troops. Fell's Point was such a hotbed of anti-Federalist sentiment that alerting the locals about the mob attack was more likely to rally more rioters than peacekeepers.

The mob scene on Charles Street had attracted angry crowds in the hundreds, but most of Fell's Point remained unaware of the growing disturbance. The Federalists' house was located in Old Town, on the other side of the Jones Falls, and many in the seafaring district commonly known as "the Point" were early risers who had retired to bed long before the violence began unfolding.

Don't Wake the "Boys from Fell's Point"

Concerns about reawakening the sleeping giant on Fell's Point weighed on the minds of those tasked with protecting the peace. Earlier in the evening, General Stricker shared his anxiety that the Charles Street house be secured before news of the rioting reached the Point. One prominent resident expressed the opinion that if "the disturbances commenced one hour earlier, or continued one hour later in the morning, the persons in the house could not have been saved, such was the prevailing temper [in Fell's Point] at the time."

With "the boys" from Fell's Point still in the dark and the cannon under control, Major Barney decided to return to General Stricker's house for an update. Stricker was in his casual clothes consulting with a handful of other men and was not pleased to see that his commanding officer had left the mob scene. Barney informed him the rioters had promised not to fire in his absence. He told the general he hoped to stall for time, "in order that the civil authority should appear, or until day-light, when I expected many of the mob would retire for fear of being recognised."

Given the unfolding violence, Barney might have expected Mayor Johnson to be on his way back to the city, but he learned that the mayor was still at his country home several miles outside Baltimore. Barney worried that if the scene dragged out too long his impatient troops would dwindle. Some were bakers and butchers whose vocations required early attention, he reminded the general. General Stricker finally said he would dispatch men to retrieve the mayor; it was around three o'clock in the morning, nearly six hours since the rioting first began.

On his return to 45 Charles Street a short time later, Major Barney realized the situation had deteriorated. One of the chief instigators was Thomas Wilson, editor of a Republican newspaper that frequently opposed Hanson. Armed with a pistol and sword, Wilson egged on the rioters and urged them to fire the cannon at the Federalists. Witnesses described him as noisy, boisterous and bloodthirsty. The men protecting the cannon had fended off Wilson's advances but could not do so much longer, so they sought out Major Barney to warn him time was running out.

But Barney's attention was distracted by another incident occurring in front of the house. An angry rioter, described as "a pale-faced young Irishman," tried to pick a fight with Andrew Boyd, the Republican who had tried to broker a peaceful solution with Hanson earlier in the night. The Irishman clearly did not appreciate Boyd's attempts to compromise with the Federalists.

"God damn you, you are as bad as they are, for by Jesus you helped to save one of them!" he yelled at Boyd and shoved him.

The Irishman drew out a rusty bayonet and tried to strike at Boyd, but Major Barney stepped between the two men. Several blows caught him on his left arm and shoulder as he worked to separate the men. There was a brief struggle, but the effort succeeded and a full-fledged brawl was averted. No sooner had Barney put out that fire then he got bad news from the men guarding the cannon.

"I was sent for by Gill," Barney recounted, "he told me, that he could no longer prevent the gun being fired, and that they had determined to allow but ten minutes more for the murderers to surrender and come out of the house."

Time was running out for Major Barney and his cavalry to prevent a massacre. There was no ticking bomb, but a loaded cannon fired from point-blank range at the Federalist house would do the job nearly as well. Barney knew he needed to stall for more time until the mayor arrived and decided it was time for a conversation with the Federalists. He approached the front passageway and was greeted with the muzzle of a musket.

"Who's that?" a voiced called out from inside the house.

"Halt, a friend, Barney—I want to see somebody," the major replied.

This prompted General Lee to come down the stairs. He approached Major Barney, who stood by the front door of the house. Barney relayed what was happening outside with the cannon and the rioters running out of patience.

"What in the name of God shall we do?" he asked.

"Major Barney, can't you dismount an officer and five or six men, and place them within the house as a guard?" Lee asked.

Barney quickly agreed. The guards would prevent any Federalists from escaping but also reduce the chance the mob would attempt to fire upon the house. "I told him that it must not appear as if this proposition came from him, or the mob would object to it," he recounted. Lee understood and explained that was why he had been cautious in speaking to the major.

The conversation ended, and Barney left the house and walked over to the cannon. He climbed on it and called out for the rioters to listen to his proposition. "I would dismount some of my men and place them with drawn swords inside the house, at the door and windows, and then nobody could escape," he said. The rioters generally liked the plan and, after brief negotiating, voiced approval. Barney asked for "three cheers" as a symbol of agreement, and the assembled mob reciprocated.

Barney stationed his lieutenant and five men in front of the house, two at each front window and another pair at the door. He gave strict orders not to let anyone other than himself in or out of the house and "if any attempted to pass to put them to death." In the rear of the property, the major stationed another four men with instructions to keep their swords raised high so they would be seen over the brick wall—and thus visible to the mob.

Since his cavalrymen had dismounted to assume their guard posts, someone needed to watch their horses. Barney asked several of the noisiest rioters to handle the reins, knowing it would give them something to do and make it less likely they would stir up trouble. The tactic worked, and several of the rioters agreed to mind the horses.

MEETING OF THE MINDS

Having successfully established the guard posts and temporarily calmed the rioters, Barney returned inside the house. One of the officers stationed in the rear yard came in with a message, and Barney followed him to the back room, where he was met by Hanson and General Lee.

Hanson was not pleased. He had observed Barney converse with the rioters since his arrival and found the major's interactions too friendly for his liking. Hanson did not share the same views as General Lee and probably disagreed with his suggestion to allow militia inside the house. The passage of night and the protracted conflict may have convinced General Lee to adopt a more conciliatory tone, but it had only hardened Hanson's resolve.

"Major Barney, what is the meaning of all this sir?" Hanson demanded. He asked why Barney had not dispersed the mob when he first had the chance. Like others in the house, Hanson felt that less speechifying and more force could have averted the present quagmire.

"I told him that I had no orders to that effect, and at any rate my force was small, there was not a single pistol among all my men," Barney replied. He expressed regret for anything derogatory he might have said but assured Hanson it was for his own safety. "I talk otherwise to deceive the mob," he said. The explanation appeared to satisfy Hanson for the moment.

Barney turned to General Lee and expressed a similar sentiment. He told the general he was placed in a "very awkward and delicate situation" and hoped any harsh words spoken would not be misinterpreted.

Grog, a mixture of rum and water, was a staple for American and British sailors. We can thank, or blame, British admiral Edward "Old Grog" Vernon for inventing the drink in the 1700s. By watering down the rum, the admiral was able to dilute rations for his sailors accustomed to their daily dose of spirits. Vernon was known as "Old Grog" because he often wore a grogram cloak (a coarse fabric made of silk and mohair), and the drink took on his nickname. *From* Songs, Naval and National, of the Late Charles Dibdin; With a Memoir and Addenda.

"Certainly not sir," Lee replied. "I know your situation; it is a delicate one. I am sure you are doing all you can, and rest assured that nothing that you may have said will operate against you."

Having mended fences with the Federalists, Barney exited the house and returned to the front of Charles Street. The sun was starting to break, and the number of rioters was increasing. One of the men passed him a cup of "very strong" grog, a traditional drink of diluted rum.

"I felt almost exhausted, but I tasted very little of it," he recalled.

The Federalists too were exhausted. They expected that the posting of guards inside the house would cause the mob to disperse, just as they expected Major's Barney's arrival with the cavalry earlier in the night would have scared off the mob. Neither action had succeeded, and now frustrations were mounting. The Federalist position was well defended, but the men were pinned down in the house and cut off from supplies.

Lee's plan to adopt a strong defensive position, hold fire and wait for the military or civil authorities to intercede was not working as hoped. The relative might of the militia, the will of the civil authority and the passion of the rioters had all been miscalculated. And the mob itself—lawless, leaderless and proletarian—was of a different sort than Lee had encountered in the past. Traditional tactics had failed, and the standoff showed no signs of abating. The ranks of the mob had indeed diminished during the middle of the night, but now they had returned in greater number. Both sides knew the cannon could not be held off indefinitely, and once word of the uprising reached all of Fell's Point in the morning, the ranks of the mob would surely swell further.

With the sun poking up Tuesday morning, the Federalists looked to an unlikely ally to help them navigate the quagmire. At long last, Mayor Edward Johnson returned from his country slumber.

8

RUNNING THE GAUNTLET

We were compelled to endure every species of contumely, insult and indignity.

T UESDAY 6:00 a.m.—Alexander Hanson was indignant. The idea of being transported to the local jail for "safekeeping" felt like a capitulation, but that was the offer on the table. It was sunup Tuesday, and not even twenty-four hours had passed since the new edition of the *Federal Republican* first hit the streets.

Mayor Edward Johnson had returned from the countryside to find his city in crisis. "The multitude were exasperated to madness," General Stricker warned him on his arrival. After speaking briefly to militia leaders and some of the rioters stationed near the cannon, the mayor led a small contingent inside the Federalists' house. Joining him were General Stricker, John Montgomery (attorney general of Maryland), Judge John Scott and a few militia officers. The city leaders acknowledged they could do little to control the rioters and pleaded with the Federalists for a peaceful surrender.

"My only object is to save the effusion of blood, and to extricate you from your present situation," Mayor Johnson told Hanson and General Lee. He explained that it would be impossible to defend the house for a sustained period of time given the growing exasperation of the rioters and the overwhelmingly negative public sentiment toward the Federalists in the city. The mob could storm the house at any moment, he warned.

The mayor offered to escort the Federalists to the city jail under militia guard. It would be a place of safety, he assured them, where Hanson's men would be better protected until they could be released on bail, presumably after the mob had disbanded. Hanson could even choose for himself who would serve as his guards, the mayor said. General Stricker added his support for the plan.

But Hanson could barely contain his contempt: "To jail…for what? For protecting my person and property against a Mob who assailed both for three hours without being fired upon when he could have killed numbers of them." He had little confidence in either Mayor Johnson or General Stricker and wasn't shy about making it known.

He continued, "It is your duty to disperse the Mob, and if you cannot disperse them, you cannot protect us to jail or after we are in jail."

General Stricker was disappointed in Hanson's response and his tone, but rather than confront him, he and Mayor Johnson decided to change tactics. Both men recognized that General Lee was more inclined to be cooperative and perhaps could be convinced to prevail upon his fellow Federalists to choose the safer way out.

The men walked into the front room to speak with Lee alone. Stricker extended his hand. "By God, Mr. Hanson does me great injustice," he exclaimed. "Gen. Lee, you are a soldier, and know the value of a soldier's word. I pledge you my word and honour as a soldier, that I will protect you to the utmost of my power, until you are out of danger from this mob."

All along, Lee and Hanson had butted heads on strategy. The veteran preached patience, while the young man in a hurry had anything but. Now events were coming to a head. At heart, Lee was a company man; he had faith in the system. Give the civil authority time to act and it will protect us, he reasoned. Lee saw his job as defending a house, while Hanson believed he was defending a principle. The difference in motivations informed their actions and widened the rift.

Mayor Johnson conversed with Lee, but the general didn't need much convincing; he agreed that the offer to surrender under militia protection was the best option they had. Lee shared his disappointment that the situation had devolved into the current standoff and made sure the mayor knew how much worse it might have been if he hadn't been present to restrain the young Federalists. He had "never entertained the idea of resisting the civil authority," Lee assured them, and expressed faith in the word and honor of General Stricker. He downplayed his own role in Hanson's plan and said his presence in the house was by accident, "that he came there by invitation to play a game of whist," the mayor recalled.

Hanson remained defiant and counseled his Federalist friends not to surrender. The city leaders were not to be trusted, he said. After all, if they could not even disperse a mob, how could they be counted on to offer protection? "He repeated over and over that if they surrendered they would all be sacrificed…massacred either on the way to jail or in the jail," one witness recounted.

Mayor Johnson and General Stricker tried to allay his suspicions. They repeatedly offered "solemn assurances" and reiterated their pledge to protect the Federalists at all costs.

"I will go with you and share your fate," the Mayor said.

Hanson dismissed the gesture. "[The mayor] will be safe enough while we will be torn to pieces," he said. "You must know that I shall be shot before I walk twenty yards," he added.

Lee remained convinced there was no other choice. He asked the city leaders for more favorable terms of surrender and suggested the Federalists be allowed to march out armed with weapons and riding on horses and in carriages. The mayor and General Stricker agreed to go outside and consult the mob to see what terms could be negotiated.

In their absence, Hanson continued to argue against surrender, while Lee tried to convince him otherwise. The house was divided. Most of the Federalists were loyal to Hanson, their contemporary and, for many, their friend. Opposing the war and defending the liberty of the press was a cause they shared—though few perhaps as fervently as Hanson himself. But Lee was the commanding officer, the war hero who had served with George Washington. For all his daring and bravado, Hanson remained a cocky twenty-six-year-old newspaper editor bumping heads with a decorated military general twice his age. The balance was tipping in Lee's direction.

Their situation was growing desperate. The number of men in the house had dwindled to about twenty, barely enough to man all the defensive stations. Fatigue had set in. Food and water rations were dwindling, and resupply would be difficult, if not impossible. The men were boxed in with no relief in sight. The attackers, on the other hand, were increasing in strength, and once word fully spread around Fell's Point, the mob would grow even more dangerous.

The solemn pledge from General Stricker also held sway with Lee. As a fellow general, he placed great faith in his honor. One man was a Federalist, the other a Republican, but they shared the same military code. Lee refused to believe that Stricker could "abandon those who surrendered their arms on the faith of his word." He warned Hanson that he was letting his prejudices get the best of him and implored the Federalists to accept a peaceful surrender.

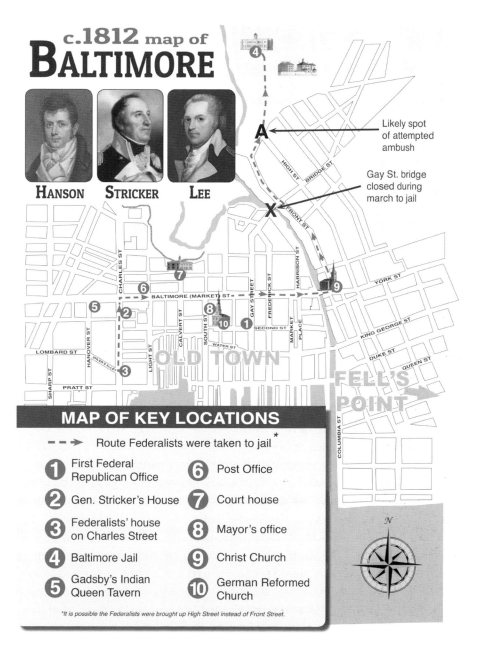

This map was created by the author based on the 1804 Hanna and Warner Plan of the city of Baltimore from the Library of Congress. Items are not drawn to scale.

"It is impossible we can be deceived after such solemn pledges for our safety," General Lee said.

"General Lee you do not know of what materials those men are composed, there is no confidence to be placed in them," Hanson countered. "Let us defend the house to the last extremity." He told the men it would be better to go down with the ship than to be dragged in the streets and likely face a massacre at the hands of the mob. He knew he'd lost the argument, but Hanson still refused to acquiesce. Instead, he suggested an alternative: allow the Federalists to hold the mayor or General Stricker hostage to assure their safety; or failing that, he would surrender just himself to appease the mob and let the others go free.

Such talk was quickly quashed by General Stricker and Mayor Johnson. Upon their return inside the house after repeated negotiations, the men delivered the bad news: the mob would brook no change in terms and no compromise other than surrender to the jail. They urged the Federalists to accept the deal as presented and warned that a delay of even five minutes "might be fatal."

The Federalists realized they were in a poor bargaining position and reluctantly agreed to the offer, despite Hanson's objections. "We had set up the whole night, had nothing to eat, and were worn down with fatigue, and found it necessary to capitulate on some terms," one of the Federalists later acknowledged.

EXITING THE HOUSE

Agreeing to the terms of surrender was one matter, actually carrying them out was quite another. Getting the Federalists safely out of the house and transported to the jail without incident would not be without peril. The mob leaders had agreed to the deal—as one-sided as it might have seemed to the Federalists—but they were hardly operating within a unified chain of command. A handful of rogue rioters taking potshots at the Federalist prisoners could be enough to scuttle the deal and wrench the city into greater chaos. Even before he exited the house, Mayor Johnson spotted trouble outside through the backyard window.

"I saw two of the militia with muskets, cross-belts and cartridge boxes, present their pieces, and deliberately take aim to shoot the first person that appeared at the window," the mayor recounted. "I immediately ran to them, and asked them what they were about."

The men said they wished to avenge their slain comrades.

"You must not do so—they are my prisoners, they have surrendered to the civil authority; we must and will protect them," the mayor commanded.

Outside the house preparations were underway. The militia had formed a hollow square with two lines of infantry and a smaller group of cavalry posted in front and rear. Led by Major Barney, they moved into position in front of the brick house and formed a lane about three feet wide. Barney posted guards at each side of the front door where the Federalists would exit the house. They were armed with German rifles fitted with bayonets and given orders to stick anyone who attempted to interfere.

The mob had grown restless during the time city leaders huddled inside the house negotiating. Suspicions and rumors abounded. Some rioters believed that the Federalists were trying to escape or that they would be taken to the jail and then immediately be bailed out. There was chatter that General Stricker and the mayor had been detained as hostages inside.

John Gill, the militia member and mob leader who had guarded the cannon, approached the front door and greeted Major Barney in an excited state. He had just learned that the Federalists were about to be escorted out of the house.

"Now I'll see the murderers—now I'll see the damn'd Tory that shot my friend Williams," he exclaimed, referring to a stonecutter named John Williams, who had been mortally injured by Federalist fire the night before.

But even in his agitated state, Gill's manner was obsequious. He shook Barney's hand and asked if it was acceptable for him to stand there. "I won't say a word to any of them, nor will I do any thing that's wrong," he pledged. "These damn'd Tories are now in the hands of the law and I am satisfied, but I know, the one that shot Williams, he had a white hat on. I know him well."

On hearing about the man in a white hat, an alarm bell went off for Major Barney, and he promptly went inside the house and advised any Federalists wearing a white hat to take it off. The Federalists already had targets on their backs, and there was no need to provide a bull's-eye.

A short time later, the call came out for more volunteers to beef up the militia escort. General Stricker asked that "respectable citizens" join them in protecting the prisoners, as the existing defense was deemed insufficient. He asked Barney to help twist arms and recruit more men, but many were reluctant to get involved, including Gill.

"Now Major Barney, what shall I do?" Gill asked. "Must I go and protect the very men who murdered my friend? I'll do whatever you tell me."

"I told him to go into the square, that he had behaved like a man all night, and that he must continue to act like one, and go into the square," Barney recalled replying.

Gill heeded the advice and marched into the hollow square formed by the militia troops. He grabbed a sword and quickly took charge, just as he had done before in commanding the cannon.

"Now lads, I will protect the murderers myself—they shall not be injured; and I tell you what, I'll kill any one of you who attempts to injure them—you are all my friends, therefore I hope you'll mind me," Gill said. Major Barney had converted a potential enemy into a useful ally for the second time.

The Federalists shuffled out of the house, escorted by the mayor, General Stricker and a handful of city leaders. The clamoring crowd immediately rushed forward, pushing and shoving and tossing rocks and insults. Stricker warned the assembled protesters that the Federalists were now under city protection and any attempt to interfere would be met harshly. He grabbed the collar of one mob member and threatened to put him to death if he tried to assault any of the prisoners. Even so, a number of rioters tried to take swipes at the men as they exited the house. Daniel Murray, Hanson's brother-in-law, was struck with a sword by one rioter.

After some tense moments, the Federalists made their way into the relative safety of the hollow square formed by the militia. The infantry closed in around them with Major Barney's cavalry flanked to the sides. An extra layer of volunteer guards acted as a buffer. Inside, there were about twenty Federalists in all, joined by Mayor Johnson, General Stricker and Attorney General John Montgomery. Surrounding them was a crowd that had swelled to two thousand or more. Most of the Federalists walked and some went in carts, but the mob would not allow any to ride in carriages.

AWAITING AN AMBUSH

It was now between eight and nine o'clock in the morning. The march to the city jail was just about a mile, but the journey was fraught with peril. It was broad daylight, and the Federalists would have to march down Charles Street, head east past the markets, cross over the Jones Falls and head north to the jail. There were several bottlenecks along the way, and the route would bring them closer to Fell's Point and the hub of hostilities.

As the procession got underway, the militia escorts worked to repel the pressing crowds; Major Barney used his sword point liberally to keep the rioters in check and the hollowed square intact. The ominous sounds of a drum and fife were heard in the crowd. Hanson was the focus of much of the anger, but all the Federalists felt the crowd's antagonism. "We were compelled to endure every species of contumely, insult and indignity," Otho Sprigg, a Federalist, recalled.[40]

While the parade of defenders marched up Charles Street, another company of men left Fell's Point with far different motivations. Once word of the negotiations with the Federalists first leaked out, the men had assembled in the yard of a local inn to hatch plans for an ambush. They knew the likely route the Federalists would take and planned an assault on the east side of the Jones Falls at the site of a vacant lot. A large pile of paving stones was stockpiled nearby for a road project and would serve as useful projectiles. Led by a local blacksmith and militia leader named Thomas Worel, the men from Fell's Point planned to drive off the militia escorts with the stones and then move in and kill the prisoners. As soon as they got word the Federalists were en route, the men rushed out to execute their plan.

Meanwhile, the Federalists continued their slow advance. They swung east onto Market Street, a wider street and one of the main thoroughfares of Old Town. Behind them was located the Indian Queen Hotel, home of Gadsby's Tavern, the popular militia hangout. Ahead, they would soon pass by the livery stables at the horse market, which was closed this morning. On Tuesdays, the market action shifted to the west end of the city at the Lexington Markets; there butchers and fishmongers offered their wares and the pungent aroma of salted cod often fill the air.[41] But this morning, it was the smell of blood that consumed the thoughts of much of the crowd.

One excited young man, identified only as Vanwyck, rode toward the scene. As the Federalists reached the next block, he remarked to one witness, "There would be fine fun, as a large company was coming from the Point to seize the persons and to put them to death."

While the Fell's Point gang raced to their rendezvous, Major Barney led his militia troops and the Federalists over the Market Street bridge spanning the Jones Falls. The swarm of rioters surrounding them tried to push the scrum rightward, in the direction of Fell's Point, but the route to the jail lay to the left. Barney barked out orders to his officers, and the chaotic mass of men slowly veered in the correct direction. They passed several houses and eventually arrived at a clearing near a vacant lot where heaps of paving stones could be seen.

The Centre Market in Old Town, running roughly parallel to the Jones Falls, was the largest market in the city and a popular spot for meats, vegetables, coffee and other products. Image by J.H. Latrobe. *Johns Hopkins University.*

The Federalists had reached the spot for the ambush. The Fell's Point gang had not.

The assassins were tardy and not in position when their prey arrived. By a matter of minutes, the plan was thwarted, but that didn't prevent the men from taking out their frustrations. They launched some paver stones at the center of the crowd and injured a few of the Federalists. One struck Charles Kilgour in the forehead, giving him a deep cut. Another Federalist was knocked to his knees. General Sticker was struck in the chest with a rock that had been marked for Hanson, and Mayor Johnson had a projectile pass within inches of his head.

Still, the escort party escaped major injury, and they shortly arrived in front of the jail. Major Barney flanked his cavalry to the sides, around the infantry, and the Federalists were able to safely make their way inside the walls of the jail. City leaders considered the effort a success. They had transported the band of Federalists from the house without any reported loss of life, despite running a perilous gauntlet surrounded by hostile crowds. Now the men were deposited in the jail and would be safely ensconced behind thick walls, heavy doors and iron bars.

A crisis had been averted. But if Mayor Johnson and General Stricker thought they could now rest easy, they were mistaken. The ambush from the Fell's Point gang had been averted, but the mob was not finished. One witness later recounted the chilling words of a mob leader, who, upon hearing that the Federalists had safely arrived at the jail, coolly remarked: "It is only a short delay, for we shall take them out of the jail tonight and put them to death."

9

BEHIND BARS WITH THE BUTCHERS

We suspected their intentions were not good.

Tuesday Morning—The "new" Baltimore Jail was perched on the east bank of the Jones Falls, overlooking much of Old Town. Next door was the Maryland penitentiary, a more utilitarian-looking structure that had been open less than a year. A high stone wall separated the two facilities on the six-acre parcel. Gallows set up in the courtyard of the jail served as a useful reminder to inmates and would-be guests.

While the state penitentiary housed hardened convicts, the city jail was for common criminals. Given the prevailing sentiment of the day in Baltimore, the Federalists might have considered themselves lucky not to be lumped in with the former. Upon their arrival, the jail keeper, John H. Bentley, led the Federalists through the lobby of the rectangular building, where a series of cells or "criminal apartments" connected via a common passageway. The men were escorted into a twenty-square-foot Spartan cell with a bare oak floor and a pair of stools. The outer door had a grating composed of thick iron bars allowing the prisoners to see out. Once inside, the Federalists breathed a sigh of relief.

"I assure you I never entered a place with a more bounding step, or lighter heart than I did these unhallowed cells," one prisoner said.

Before departing, Mayor Johnson and General Stricker repeated their assurances and pledged protection for the prisoners. There were two dozen Federalists in all: Hanson, General Lee, General Lingan, Otho Sprigg, John

The Baltimore Jail featured three levels with small round windows ranging along the top, curved parapet walls and a cupola planted in the center. Gothic features were incorporated into the design to give the facility an authoritative look. Poppleton Map. *Library of Congress.*

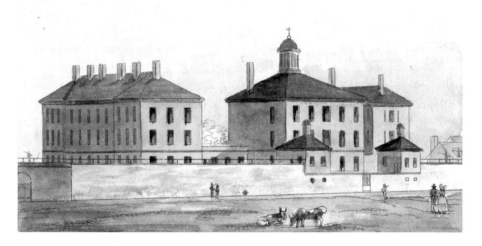

Next to the jail sat the Maryland Penitentiary. Until the penitentiary was opened, convicted felons often served out their time in chain gangs laboring on public road projects, under a practice known as "wheelbarrow law." The penitentiary was thought of as a more humane and reform-minded approach. It also avoided the spectacle of having criminals toiling about city streets and the unintended consequences that sometimes went along. The inmates seemed to have agreed. When the penitentiary first opened, there were fifty-four convicts. All were given a choice of fates, and forty-seven elected to serve their time in the penitentiary rather than on the roads. Maryland was one of the first states to adopt this more progressive view of penal reform. Poppleton Map. *Library of Congress.*

Thompson, Daniel Murray (Hanson's brother-in-law), Ephraim Gaither, William Gaither, John Hall, Peregrine Warfield, Charles Kilgore, David Hoffman and a dozen others.

A few of the men had suffered injuries during the Charles Street standoff. The most seriously injured was Ephraim Gaither, who was wounded by musket fire during the night. He lost a considerable amount of blood and later had a convulsion. One of his brothers brought him upstairs to rest in the bed, and he was able to make it to the jail, probably delivered in a cart. Ephraim shared the cell with his brother William; the third Gaither brother, Henry, managed to sneak away during the procession to the jail and left the city.

It was close to ten o'clock in the morning on Tuesday by the time all in the group finally settled in their cells. Most of the men had been up all night, and they were hungry and fatigued. In spite of the bare floor and dungeon-like atmosphere, a number seized the opportunity to sleep.

MORE CHAOS ON CHARLES STREET

Outside the jail, Major Barney had dismissed his cavalry troops and ridden back into town. He dismounted from his horse in front of General Stricker's house on Charles Street and walked over to the Federalist house a few doors down. A raucous crowd congregated outside, still in search of blood. Inside the house, vandals were destroying the furniture, dismantling doors and closets and throwing items out of the window. One man, possibly the landlord's son, tried to prevent the destruction, but his efforts were ignored. A similar scene played out nearby at the family home of Hanson's newspaper partner, Jacob Wagner.

Seeing there was little he could do, Barney left and returned to the home of General Stricker, who was in a much better mood this time; the Federalists had been successfully escorted to the jail, and the massive mob near his home had been restrained.

"He thanked me for my conduct and exertions and, almost sobbing, said, 'You have saved the lives of perhaps hundreds,'" Barney recalled. "My God! What would have been the consequences if you had not gone down," Stricker told him.

After a brief conversation with the general, Major Barney left to grab a late breakfast. Then, with the peace of the city seemingly restored—at least temporarily—Barney decided to head home for a change of clothes and a quick nap.

The activity at the Charles Street house continued. At one point during the day, a rumor circulated that one of the Federalists had hidden himself inside the chimney. The prospect of capturing one of Hanson's men must have been tantalizing, and the vandals scrambled into action. A small group climbed the roof of the house with the intention of throwing rocks down the chimney flue from above to dislodge the man, according to one spectator who later recounted the story in his local newspaper. The plan may not have been well-coordinated, however, as another man decided to climb up the chimney from inside the house in order to grab the target and drag him down from below.

"While playing at his game of *peep devil*, his worship below had a very uncivil salutation from a brickbat…visited his head and shoulders with some hard knocks and his whole dress with a sable shower of soot," the newspaper reported. The comedy of errors quickly turned more serious, as the man below, now covered with soot, was mistaken for a hidden Federalist. The mob knocked him around, clawed at his coat and forced him to flee to a local tavern, where he cleaned his face. Eventually, his real identity was discovered, and "the patriotic band returned to the destruction of the enemy's property, with renewed animation."[42]

Enter Judge Scott

A short distance away, near the courthouse, a small group of Federalist supporters was making a case for bail to Judge John Scott. A portly man of forty-four who suffered from health issues that hindered his ability to walk for any distance, Judge Scott was the chief justice of the criminal court and a Republican loyalist. He had been appointed in 1808 after losing a race for Congress and serving a term in the state assembly.

Judge Scott had been present on Charles Street earlier in the morning when the Federalists surrendered and earlier in the night had paid a visit inside the house in an attempt to negotiate a peaceful outcome. Once the men were deposited into the jail, their fate fell largely into his hands, as the mayor had not left any formal instructions and there was some question as to their legal status. In the morning, the judge ordered the sheriff to detain the men until "legally discharged." What that meant was a matter of discussion.

Around eleven o'clock Tuesday morning, the Federalist supporters visited the chief justice on behalf of their friends in jail. Among the petitioners was, coincidentally, Judge Scott's predecessor as chief justice, Walter Dorsey, a man who had some experience with the politics of mobs. Dorsey and his colleagues asked the judge to allow their Federalist friends to be released from on bail. Judge Scott may have initially agreed, but he soon changed his mind and turned down the application.

He may have been influenced by the presence of Mayor Johnson's attorney, John Purviance, who arrived late to the discussion and advised against the prisoners' release. Purviance believed the jail was the safest place for the Federalists. "If they were admitted to bail, they would have fallen sacrifices to the fury of an insatiate mob," he told the judge.

There was also the matter of criminal charges. The death of the French mob leader, Dr. Gale, triggered an inquest to determine the cause of death. The results were reported to Judge Scott quickly, charging those in the Charles Street house guilty of "willful murder." Even if the prisoners' safety were not at issue, the men would have to answer for the murder charge, and left unsaid was the fact that Judge Scott himself would have to answer to the mob if the prisoners were released prematurely.

Bail might be out of the question, but Judge Scott looked upon another request more favorably. Dorsey and his Federalist colleagues asked the judge to take steps to boost the guard detail at the jail. The mob had quieted after Hanson's gang was secured inside, but by midday, the chatter had returned and many expected the mob soon to follow. The men feared for their friends' safety. One Federalist attorney present minced no words: "It was manifest from the threats of the mob, that it was their intention to break the jail to get at the prisoners and murder them," he told the judge.

John Purviance recognized the danger as well and voiced his support, but Attorney General John Montgomery objected. He did not think it proper to call up the militia. Mayor Johnson arrived a bit later to the meeting after attending to some matters in his own office. He eventually agreed, and the men jointly decided to draft a formal order calling out the militia to protect the jail.

Militia Called Out Again

The mayor took up a pen and began to write out the order. He appreciated the need to protect the prisoners but remained skeptical about the role of the militia, which had a propensity for causing trouble as often as it solved it. While writing the order, the mayor's hand began to shake, perhaps in a manifestation of his anxieties. Seeing his visible tremor, Purviance stepped in and drew up the order for him with the appropriate legal language. The mayor did not make any mention of the incident in his later report, indicating that he may have felt some embarrassment.

After a short time, the paper was signed and the meeting broke up. Mayor Johnson and his team departed to deliver the militia order to General Stricker. Once he was outside and alone with his advisors, the mayor voiced his reservations about the action they were about to take.

"Gentlemen, hear my predictions. God grant they may not be verified—there is no confidence to be placed in the militia; they will not obey the call. They will not turn out," he said, "and if you depend upon them I fear you will be disappointed."

Major Barney for one was disappointed to hear the news a short time later. He had changed his clothes but never did get his nap. Now he was back on Charles Street, and General Stricker was ordering him to mobilize again. He knew his men were weary and fatigued; they had been up all night. Barney asked if the general might call up one of the other militia companies instead.

"No, I know you must be fatigued, but you can manage the mob," General Stricker replied.

Stricker displayed more faith in Major Barney than many of his other commanding officers. He did order up an artillery company and the Fifth Infantry Regiment to bolster Major Barney's cavalry, but General Stricker asked his infantry field officer, Colonel Joseph Sterett, not to issue ball cartridges to the troops. He did not want them to have live ammunition. Whether this was an order or a recommendation is unclear. Sterett later described it as a verbal order.

Apart from Major Barney, a loyal Republican, most of the staff officers ordered to muster their troops were Federalists. General Stricker could have called up any number of regiments; why he chose primarily Federalists field officers is a matter of conjecture. He may have believed that regiments led by Federalist officers would be better motivated to defend the jail. He may also have believed, some later testified, that Colonel Sterett's Fifth Regiment was better trained than most. Or he may have wanted to cover his bets if the operation failed and he needed to divert the blame away from Republicans.

Whatever the motivation, the military officers were directed to muster by five o'clock that evening in the center of town. While the men went off to make preparations, Mayor Johnson and Judge Scott returned to the jail with the intent of checking in on the Federalist prisoners. The mayor likely had another motive on his mind as well; a relative of his had been mistakenly imprisoned along with the Federalists earlier in the day, and he was anxious to effect his release.

When the mayor and the judge arrived, they found a boisterous crowd gathered near the front steps of the jail. It was between two and three o'clock on Tuesday afternoon. The assemblage grew suspicious when they spotted the mayor and Judge Scott.

"We were accused with an intention improperly to bail the prisoners, with a view to rescue them from the hands of justice," Mayor Johnson recalled.

He was afraid to enter the jail, for once the front door was unlocked, the men outside might attempt to rush in with him. After they offered assurances and explained that they were not coming to transfer or bail out the Federalist prisoners, the crowd was pacified and the mayor and his party entered without further incident.

UNEXPECTED VISITORS AT THE JAIL

Bentley, the jailer, escorted Mayor Johnson, Judge Scott and several others to the Federalists' cell. Hanson and Lee had already been apprised that they would not be released on bail, but they remained worried. Rumors of another mob attack were rampant, and the security inside the jail appeared lax. Murmurs about the jailer's alleged mob sympathies also did not inspire confidence.

Earlier in the afternoon, the Federalists had asked Bentley to lock the passageway door from the outside and then pass them the key through the iron grate so they would be assured no unauthorized visitors could enter, but he refused, citing their status as prisoners. Some of the Federalists' allies outside had also taken steps on their own to press for better security. One asked the sheriff to take responsibility for holding the keys rather than entrusting them to Bentley. The sheriff declined and said he had confidence in his jailer, though privately he had heard rumors, too, and already expressed his worries about the jail security to city officials.

Once the mayor and his party arrived, General Lee asked him if he thought the Federalists could be adequately protected. He shared his concerns about making the sure the intermediate doors leading to the cells were locked and secured. In this jail, the prisoners were less concerned about trying to get out and were more worried about who might get in. The mayor offered his personal pledge that they would be secure and updated the men on the steps that had been taken so far.

"[I] told him the military had been called upon, and at any rate they might depend upon me," he said. "I would remain at the jail all night, and they never shall get at you but through me."

The conversation and the repeated assurances from the mayor appeared to ease the fears of the twenty-plus prisoners in the crowded jail cell. As he was wrapping up, one of the mayor's advisors quietly leaned in and whispered to him.

"Be cautious what you say, you are watched," he said.

The mayor cast a sweeping glance around the jail cell and spotted two men standing against the wall with hats covering part of their faces. He did not recognize either man, and their appearance "was not calculated to inspire confidence."

When he was done, Mayor Johnson stopped to speak to Bentley on his way out and questioned him about the two suspicious men. What were those "improper characters" doing inside his jail in the same cell with the prisoners, the mayor asked? The jailer replied that he couldn't help it, as the men had slipped in when the mayor's party arrived to see the Federalists. Under pressure, the jailer agreed to clear everyone out of the cells who wasn't supposed to be there and pledged to fasten the cell doors.

After receiving these assurances, the mayor exited the jail and walked into the courtyard. He found a growing crowd of restless spectators and did his best to allay their suspicions. The prisoners would not be bailed out but would be brought to trial to answer for their actions as speedily as possible, he repeated. In other words, there was no need for the crowd to take matters in its own hands.

The mayor was right to worry. The two men inside the jail cell were John Mumma and James Maxwell, both local meat butchers, and they were on a reconnaissance mission for the mob. The men entered the cell around the same time as the mayor's party—one may have even been given a key—and used the opportunity to carefully observe each of the prisoners, including their appearance and clothing.

"Mumma asked me the names of several of the prisoners," one Federalist prisoner later recalled. "We suspected their intentions were not good," he said. Mumma and Maxwell cleared out around five o'clock, but the Federalists suspected it would not be the last they'd see of them.

The butchers would be back.

10

FINAL PLEAS

It is not yet too late, support me, and we may prevent the horrid scene.

Tuesday Afternoon—The tipping point came in a familiar package: a newspaper. But this time, the article whipping up the passions of the populace was not Hanson's *Federal Republican* but a Republican newspaper published by an old nemesis. Under editor Baptis Irvine, the pages of the *Baltimore Whig* offered up rhetoric even more pointed and caustic than Hanson's. With the Federalists beaten back and locked up in jail and a feisty mob ready to pounce, Irvine used the opportunity to gin up its emotions.

His latest edition of the *Whig* was distributed around the jail yard starting Tuesday morning and could not have done more to incite the mob. While acknowledging that "no man or set of men ought to assail property or person unlawfully," the *Whig* wrote that "since a band of murderous traitors, did provoke the people, the people ought to have raised their garrison to the ground, and put them every man to death."[43]

Irvine's newspaper accused Hanson and his Federalists of being enemies to the country who had come to Baltimore with the express purpose of provoking an attack. They could easily be released on bail and have their trial removed to an adjoining county and thus avoid local justice, he warned.

Irvine had a history of taking the liberty of the press up to—and well past—the line. He and Hanson had once faced off in court on the very same principle four years prior. It was one of Hanson's first cases as an attorney,

The *Baltimore Whig* was published by Baptis Irvine, a Frenchman from Pennsylvania. *From the* Baltimore Whig.

and he did not mask his distaste for Irvine, calling the editor a "factious, hot headed, turbulent printer…who himself fattens upon the 'dead carcass' of plundered reputation."[44]

Mayor Johnson saw the *Whig* newspaper and was crestfallen. He knew his job had just grown more difficult. "I read it with great anguish and disapprobation, considering the remarks it contained were calculated to defeat my efforts to abate the violence of the mob," he said.

His worries were well founded. The newspaper was stirring unrest at a precarious time. Until the city militia arrived later, the jail was essentially unguarded save for the mayor and handful of men, and some of the city officials on hand did more harm than good, spreading the same propaganda published in the *Whig*. One high-ranking official reminded the mayor,

"You well know, Mr. Johnson, that these persons can remove their trial to Montgomery, and what sort of a trial they will have there."

True to his word, the mayor remained at the jail throughout the day. Other "respectable citizens" joined him at various times, and they mixed in with the uneasy crowd spread around the yard, doing their best to bat down rumors and calm fears. Each time he spoke, the mayor repeated his assurances that the prisoners would not be bailed and that they would stand trial as quickly as possible.

CITY MILITIA DEFECTED AND DEJECTED

Late in the afternoon, General Stricker arrived at the jail and delivered more bad news. The militia continued to defect in great numbers, and only a few dozen had turned out, despite pleas from their commanding officers. Some men cited the order not to use live ammunition, others the fear of violence—and nearly all a general distaste for protecting Federalists like Alexander Hanson—as motivation for disobeying the muster order.

Asked to explain, one militia captain summed up the feelings of the rank and file: "They were always ready and willing to meet the enemies of their country and to sacrifice their lives in its defense," he said, "but that they never would turn out to protect traitors or disorganizers, and on the present occasion declined." Another man told his commanding officer he'd sooner burn his uniform than disgrace it by turning out to protect the Federalists.

The small force that did report was currently assembling on Gay Street near the center of Old Town, a short distance from the Charles Street house. Colonel Sterett's infantry regiment turned out about thirty men, while Major Barney's cavalry managed just one; another eight or so from various regiments joined them. It was a meager showing for a brigade comprising greater than seven hundred men.

Perhaps even more concerning was a much larger crowd of spectators gathered around the militia. The muster order had seemingly stirred more men to rally against Hanson and the Federalists than come to their defense. Among them was Baptis Irvine, the *Whig* newspaper editor, who was apparently not content to merely rile readers with his words. Rumors darted through the rowdy spectators, and the gathered crowd watched the militia with keen interest.

General Stricker worried that such a paltry showing would embolden the rioters. He told the mayor he was considering ordering the militia to stand down. Parading them from Gay Street up to the jail would just draw more unwanted attention, he said, and remind the mob that the bulk of the military was on their side. The general also downplayed the likelihood of any further mischief at the jail that evening. "I found the assemblage of people had greatly diminished and was every moment decreasing," he wrote later in a report to the governor. Stricker expressed similar confidence to Sheriff William Merryman, telling him he was "not in the smallest degree apprehensive of danger."

Stricker was correct about diminishing crowds at the jail, but for the wrong reasons—a miscalculation that later would prove deadly. The rioters had no intention of giving up; they returned to town merely to size up the opposition.

After hearing the mayor on the militia question, General Stricker had seemingly reached his decision. "What do you mean to do?" he asked the mayor as he prepared to leave.

"I intend staying here all night, and if the respectable people will continue with me, we certainly shall be able to protect the jail," the mayor said.

Stricker appeared anxious. "It is hard to leave you under such circumstances. I have been up all night, and my family is in great distress, which will be increased by my absence," he said, referring to his wife and five daughters. "I do not see how I can possibly stay with you."

The mayor was sympathetic. He'd been out at his home in the country the previous night with his own family. "As you had all the fatigue and trouble of the last night, I will undertake it tonight, and do the best I can," he assured the general.

After this conversation, General Stricker departed the jail and rode back to town. On his return, he encountered his infantry commander marching toward the jail with about thirty men. The general reported that there was little danger at the jail and told Colonel Sterett and his men to retreat and await further orders. Sterett remained worried, but he obeyed the order and returned to Gay Street. Later, at about half past six, the general dismissed the men altogether; the fire bell would signal them to return if needed.

For the assembled crowd, the dismissal of the militia served as a different kind of signal. Throughout the day, the rioters had bounced from the Charles Street house up to the jail and then back to town to monitor the militia. Now, with the military standing down, they were emboldened and ready to attack. A group of about thirty or forty men, most from Fell's Point, began their march to the jail.

Supporters of the jailed Federalists were chagrined to learn of General Stricker's dismissal order. Many were convinced the mob intended to strike that evening and their friends would be murdered. Some Federalists, including Hanson's uncle, tried to organize an ad hoc force to defend the jail. Plans were made to collect swords and horses and then rendezvous at the home of a local doctor.

FELL'S POINT GANG ARRIVES

As the sun set on Tuesday evening, Mayor Johnson watched the crowd at the jail increase and the chatter about bail get louder. Just when it seemed that calm had returned, a new rumor began circulating that Bentley the jail keeper intended to open the door and give up his keys. The mayor tracked down the sheriff in the yard and dispatched him to verify that the jail doors were properly secured. He needed to know if his jailer was dependable or a "coward." The sheriff confronted Bentley, who denied any plan to give up the keys. "He declared that the report was groundless," the sheriff reported.

The mayor knew his only chance to prevent another incident that evening was to convince the crowd that the Federalists would not be released on bail. His own words of assurance had proven ineffectual so he asked an associate to quickly ride over to Judge Scott's house and get him to sign a written statement confirming he would not accept bail. The mayor hoped this would pacify the crowd.

No sooner had the mayor's aide departed then the gang from Fell's Point arrived. The men marched into the jail yard with loud hoots and hollers. They carried hatchets, clubs, crowbars and an assortment of crude weapons.

"Where are those murdering scoundrels who have come from Montgomery and slaughtered our citizens in cold blood!" cried the ringleader, a cordwainer named George Wolleslager, who carried a violent reputation.

Wolleslager had helped destroy the Federalist newspaper office during the first riot in June and may have played a role in organizing the attack. On Monday night, he joined the Charles Street rioters and later ended up in the watch house as a result. After his release in the afternoon, he joined the crowd on Gay Street, along with Baptis Irvine and others. Whatever his talents as a shoemaker, Wolleslager had a knack for stirring up trouble.

"In that jail my boys; we must have them out; blood cries for blood!" Wolleslager exclaimed as the men swarmed into the yard and headed toward the jail's entrance.

Mayor Johnson was standing nearby with a few other men. He called out and asked who was there.

"George Wolleslager," the voice replied. "Who are you?"

"A friend," the mayor replied.

"What do you want with me?"

"I wish to speak with you," the mayor said.

Wolleslager and his gang stopped, and the mayor approached. "Who are you sir?" Wolleslager asked.

"My name is Johnson, I am the mayor of your city."

"What do you want with me?" the shoemaker repeated.

"The expressions you have used give me much uneasiness," the mayor warned. "Those persons in jail are my prisoners....It is my duty to protect them, and I am here for that purpose, and I call on you to assist me in doing so."

"Mr. Johnson, what will be done with these men who are in jail?" Wolleslager asked.

"Never do you mind; they will be brought before the court," the mayor said.

"Upon your honour, Mr. Johnson!"

"Yes, upon my honour, they shall be tried," the mayor repeated.

Wolleslager proceeded to complain about the treatment he had received at the hands of the city watchmen the night before. Mayor Johnson pledged to punish any misconduct and offered to call the watchmen into his office the next morning so they could get to the bottom of it.

The conciliatory approach seemed to work, and Wolleslager's tone promptly changed. "Mr. Mayor, you talk very reasonably, and we will support, well, my boys, we will support the mayor," he said. "Three cheers for the mayor!"

For a moment, it appeared the mayor's diplomacy might avert further violence. But not all the would-be rioters were convinced, including Wolleslager's brother. A few men pulled on his jacket and called him back. Standing about ten to fifteen yards away, the mayor watched uncomfortably as the shoemaker conversed out of earshot. With him having been swayed one way by the mayor, it now appeared the men were trying to remind Wolleslager of their original mission.

The mayor could see his victory slipping away, so he walked over to them to interrupt the conversation. He offered more flattery to his new friend, telling him that "I depended upon him, that he was powerful and strong and brave, and if supported by him, had nothing to fear."

The compliment did the job, and Wolleslager repeated his support. The mayor then gestured to another large collection of men near the jail entrance who looked to be up to no good. He asked Wolleslager to walk over with him, and the shoemaker agreed.

As the two men approached, the mayor heard the group making threats on the prisoners in a low voice. One man waved a log of wood and remarked that he could easily break down the jail door. The mayor laid his hand on the man's shoulder. "I am the mayor of your city; they are my prisoners, and I must and will protect them," he said.

This crowd was not as receptive to the mayor's entreaties. Several in the group shouted back in anger. "You damn'd scoundrel don't we feed you?" asked one especially agitated man. "Is it not your duty to head and lead us on to take vengeance for the murders committed?"

Wolleslager stepped between the mayor and the angry mob. "We will protect the mayor," he said. The crowd was unmoved, and a handful of men climbed the rear steps of the jail and began hammering at the door with an axe, accompanied by loud huzzas.

Mayor Johnson implored his new friend to help: "It is not yet too late, support me, and we may prevent the horrid scene."

"I will support you sir," Wolleslager answered. He and a pair of his men pushed their way up the jail steps in an apparent effort to stop the other group from breaking in the door.

Then he stopped.

Wolleslager turned suddenly and faced the mayor. He reached out with two hands, no doubt toughened from years of stretching and shaping leather, and placed them on the mayor. There was nothing more they could do, the shoemaker advised. "We were only risking our own lives without any prospect of success," he said, according to the mayor.

The steps to the jail were narrow, and the mayor was almost pushed off. He jumped down. The men continued to hammer away at the upper panel of the jail door. With the crowd pushing forward and spiraling out of control, the mayor was grabbed on the arm by a friendly militia officer and pulled to safety. He was clearly distressed. "My God! What shall we do. I am ruined forever," he said aloud, according to one witness.

The mayor watched as the men worked to force the door open. The rioters had formed two distinct groups and now seemed to converge at the back entrance where the jail abutted the state penitentiary. The outer door was stout and withstood the blows, but then, inexplicably, the door opened. A loud cheer went up.

It was the sound of defeat for Mayor Johnson. As the rioters streamed into the jail, a weary mayor "much exhausted both in body and mind" was escorted away and led home. His ordeal was over for the night, but the Federalists' was just beginning.

11

BREAK-INS AND BREAK-OUTS

We'll rout out the damn'd Tories. We'll drink their blood. We'll eat their hearts!

TUESDAY EVENING—The brutish banging and hammering echoed throughout the jail as darkness fell. Next came the rowdy cheers, the shuffling of footsteps and the bloodcurdling yells. Alexander Hanson knew the fates had come knocking.

The window grates in the cell limited his view of the yard, but Hanson suspected the jail entrance had opened via treachery rather than force. He was already deeply suspicious of Bentley, the jailer, who had denied a request to provide arms so his Federalists could defend themselves and refused to turn over the key that secured their cell. He also suspected that Bentley had allowed the two butchers, Mumma and Maxwell, into the jail earlier in the day.

Now the rioters were inside the building. Several layers of security still protected the Federalists from the mob, including a wooden door and two iron gates. A show of force by the militia might still avert disaster, but after the mayor's capitulation, odds of a rescue appeared remote. Hanson's uncle was still rallying a defensive force, but that also might be too little too late. The Federalists knew they were running out of time.

"We were thus shut up like sheep in the pen, waiting the hand of the butcher," one prisoner recalled.

Major William Barney, the cavalry commander, returned to his home on Lexington Street after dismissing the men in his regiment. Despite his recruiting efforts, no more than a dozen reported for duty, and some came without uniforms or weapons. Based on reports from General Stricker and others, Barney assumed the military would not be needed at the jail that evening. He also must have been exhausted; it had been a whirlwind twenty-four hours since the major had been awakened from his sleep the night before, and he was looking forward to some rest.

With torches in hand and sleeves rolled up, the rioters labored to open the first outer door leading to the prisoner cell area. Using sledgehammers, they pounded away at the wood gratings in the door while Sheriff Merryman entered the jail hall with one or two other men in a last effort to prevent the attack. "We called to the people and commanded them to desist," the sheriff recounted, but his words were ignored. He described the rioters as "infuriated spirits."

HANSON AND LEE PLOT FINAL STAND

Inside the cells, the Federalists considered their options. The men were not totally defenseless; they had a pair of long daggers and several pistols among them. General Lee realized his faith in the civil authority and General Stricker had been misplaced. He had counseled restraint throughout the ordeal but now advised the men to use the few weapons on hand to shoot any rioters who breached the cell so as to "avoid falling by ignoble and dastardly hands."

Hanson immediately disagreed. He and Lee had clashed repeatedly on tactics and strategy since the first stone was launched at nightfall on Monday—a mere twenty-four hours earlier by the clock—and now, as the Federalists prepared for their last stand, the relationship was no different. Hanson argued that it would be useless to kill one or two men in a sea of rioters. It would only enrage them further and make escape more difficult. Instead, Hanson detailed an alternative plan; this time, General Lee readily agreed.

—Bam! The rioters smashed through the wood grating and shouted in excitement. Iron bars were next. Using crowbars, the men strained to bend the rods. Others chipped at the brick wall holding the lock. The scrape of metal and the creaking of wood audibly warned of the mob's approach.

Still, the mood among the Federalists remained upbeat, even though most had not slept in more than thirty-six hours. "They were cheerful, conversable and sometimes gay," Hanson later reported. Unlike most of the prisoners who typically occupied the cells of the Baltimore Jail, Hanson and most of his cohorts were motivated by principle, which so far had proved a unifying force.

"Not even when the forcing of the jail door was announced by the savage yell of the Mob…was there a look, a whisper, or motion of the body, expressive of any thing but cool, collected courage and contempt of death," Hanson wrote.

For the rioters, the iron door presented more of an obstacle than the wood grating, but after about half an hour the men broke through. Huzzas and cries of "Tory!" filled the air. They were now inside the common hallway adjacent to the individual jail cells. One iron cell door was now all that separated the mob from the Federalists.

Having no success dissuading rioters inside the jail, Sheriff Merryman returned outside and decided to ride into town to alert Judge Scott. It was about eight o'clock when he arrived at the judge's house on St. Paul's Lane, a short distance from the courthouse. He promptly updated the judge about the break-in at the jail, warning that "without immediate assistance there would be murder." Judge Scott ordered the fire bell rung and summoned a posse comitatus to assist. He then directed the sheriff to track down General Stricker. The sheriff complied and promptly rode off to find General Stricker, alerting any men he encountered in the streets to rally at the courthouse.

The rioters swarmed in and pushed through the passageway. They stopped first at the cell opposite the Federalists. One of the men inside was Otho Sprigg, who had quietly switched cells earlier in the day and now mixed in "among the dregs of society" with five other common prisoners, including a Frenchman. To avoid detection, Sprigg disguised himself by wearing a red handkerchief over his neck, a white handkerchief around his head and a different color coat. The ruse worked, and the rioters did not recognize him. If Sprigg felt any remorse for abandoning his Federalist colleagues, he did not show it. "Self-preservation is a powerful stimulus to invention," he later explained.

The rioters struck at the cell door three times with an axe or hatchet before realizing they were at the wrong spot. They were aided by none other than Hanson's brother-in-law Daniel Murray. "You are at the wrong door—here we are," he called out from across the hall. The area was illuminated by torchlight and oil lamps in the passageway. Upon realizing their mistake, the rioters' tone toward the men in the "dregs" cell promptly changed; these prisoners were not Federalist enemies but apparently Republican allies.

"When the Mob discovered they were at the wrong door, they squeezed my hand with great cordiality, and promised me a speedy liberation from confinement," Sprigg recalled.

The Federalists' final layer of protection was the iron door to their cell. It was locked and, without the key, would not be easily forced open. Murray and another man standing inside the door held up their pistols. "My lads you had better retire; we shall shoot some of you," one warned. Hanson and Lee reminded the men of their plan and advised them not to fire at the rioters.

As the drama neared a crescendo at the jail, Sheriff Merryman tried to track down General Stricker. He rode from the judge's house over to Charles Street where the general lived, but got no answer. Around the same time, friends of the Federalists, led by Hanson's uncle, met at the agreed upon location at the home of a local doctor to form a defensive force. But the forty men who had originally agreed to mount up with broadswords in hand turned out to be only four.

At his home in town, Major Barney was stirred by the sound of the bell ringing, but it did not sound like a regular fire bell, he thought. It was around nine o'clock. Barney went to the attic of his house for a better look, but he didn't see anything or hear any unusual noise. Still, he suspected another mob attack and went outside to investigate.

FEDERALISTS READY FOR ONSLAUGHT

Inside the cell, the Federalists readied for the onslaught. The room was not large, and there were as many as twenty men packed inside. They expected the iron door would afford some extra time—and perhaps even a last-ditch chance for help to arrive—but those hopes were dashed when the locked door abruptly swung open. The rioters had the key. Some witnesses would later claim Bentley opened the door; others suspected Mumma, the butcher.

In either case, the Federalists were ready. "As there was no means of escape we prepared for the event with fortitude," one Federalist recalled. Daniel Murray, a former naval officer, and a man named John Thompson rushed out of the cell first. They were chosen because they were considered the strongest men of the group. Their assignment was to create confusion and extinguish the lights while the rest of the men would follow behind, and amid the bedlam to follow, it was hoped many could escape into the crowd.

Hanson understood that he would not be spared; the rioters would surely recognize him. But many of his cohorts might be not be, and he hoped to allow as many as possible to escape. If they had fired the pistols, as some of the Federalists desired, Hanson knew they could have killed one or two rioters, but a dozen more stand-ins stood ready to replace the fallen, and any provocation would enrage the mob further and make the escape more difficult.

The plan worked to a degree. While the rioters scuffled with some of the Federalists by the cell door entrance, many were able to navigate down the passageway toward the jail lobby in the chaos. The rioters had trouble seeing and called out for more candles. Hanson himself made his way out of the cell and into the dim corridor. He approached the iron door on the way to the lobby and stopped in his tracks.

Looking up, he saw the tall and muscular figure of Mumma, the butcher, standing guard by the gate. Hanson felt a blow to his head and was knocked to the ground. Many of the other Federalists who rushed out met the same fate. The purpose of the butcher's presence in the cell earlier in the day was now apparent. Mumma was tasked with identifying each Federalist as he exited, giving each victim a blow with a club or his fist to "designate them for slaughter." A gang of rioters stood nearby ready to finish the job the butcher had started.

The sounds of a drum and fife could be heard coming from the yard. Outside, the chants had begun. "We'll rout out the damn'd Tories. We'll drink their blood. We'll eat their hearts."[45]

The massacre was on.

12

THE MASSACRE

Are you not sick at the recital of this shocking affair?

TUESDAY EVENING—James M. Lingan was no stranger to the brutality of jail. He'd spent much of the American Revolution on a British prison ship after being captured in battle. Confined under horrific conditions in a space too small for him to stand fully up or lie down flat, Lingan nonetheless turned down a sizeable monetary offer (including the rank of a British army officer) to switch sides. "I'll rot here first," he reportedly responded to his British captors.[46] His captivity had a lasting impact; it was months before Lingan could sleep in anything other than an armchair. After the war, he returned to Georgetown and served as a port collector and was later promoted to the rank of brigadier general in the militia.

In many respects, General Lingan, aged sixty-one, was the silent partner in Hanson's "Spartan Band." Described as stout man of imposing stature, Lingan shared Hanson's devotion to the Federalist cause, but not his fiery temperament. He was a quiet family man with an "affectionate and sympathizing heart." Lingan was a friend of Hanson's and actively supported the *Federal Republican*, though his actual role with the newspaper is unclear. He may have owned a partial stake in the paper.[47]

While Hanson and Lee had clashed repeatedly since the Federalists returned to Charles Street, Lingan avoided the limelight and instead exerted a calming influence on the group. His status as a war hero brought gravitas to the effort, but he largely deferred to Lee on military tactics and to Hanson on political matters.

General James Lingan, who had heroically faced down the British during the Revolutionary War, now stood accused by the mob of being an anti-war British sympathizer. *Library of Congress.*

For the mob, Lingan was just another target of their wrath. As Lingan hustled out of the Federalist jail cell, he was spotted by the mob and knocked down, probably by Mumma. He was dragged to the front entrance of the jail and pitched down the narrow stairs exiting the building. There a gang of rioters circled around him, waving clubs and swatting at him each time he tried to rise. The general was quickly covered in bruises. As the sanguinary scene unfolded in the yard in front of the jail, one sympathetic spectator tried to intervene.

"I entreated them not to kill an old man, the father of a number of helpless children; one who had fought in defense of the freedom of our country," implored William Gywnn, the Federalist attorney.

The plea went unheeded.

"He is one of those damn'd rascals who came from a distance to murder our citizens," said one assailant. "No matter what he was formerly, he is a damn'd Tory now, he ought to be put to death."

As the rioters continued to shower Lingan with blows, many of his Federalist counterparts were suffering a similar reception. A few were able to sneak through the crowds, but Mumma's identification protocol was proving ruthlessly efficient. Splattered blood on the ground, tattered remnants of clothing and a bloody handprint on the wall marked the trail of violence.

MORE FEDERALISTS IN MOB CROSSHAIRS

One of the first victims was John Thompson, a local Baltimore resident who had joined the Federalists at the Charles Street house on Monday evening at Hanson's invitation. When they made their break, Thompson rushed out of the jail cell into the hall passageway. He got as far as the outer door when he was struck on the head with a club. The force of the blow carried him forward, and he fell down the front step, tumbling about twelve feet to the ground.

"There I saw a gang of ruffians armed with clubs ready to destroy whomsoever should pass down the steps, and six or seven of them instantly assaulted me while down, and beat me about the head until I was unable to rise," Thompson recounted.

He was dragged another twenty or thirty yards away from the entrance and pummeled with more clubs and sticks. One of the mayor's associates who had remained at the scene spotted Thompson and tried to convince his attackers to relent, but, as with Lingan, the mob was in no mood to negotiate. Instead, it was decided that Thompson should be tarred and feathered. The sentence having been handed out, a handful of rioters carrying torches went off in search of tar with a beaten-up Thompson dragged in tow.

Following close behind Thompson when he exited the jail cell was another local Federalist, John Hall, an attorney and friend of Hanson's. When he first arrived at the Charles Street house Monday morning, Hall had joked with Hanson about his penchant for stirring up trouble, telling his friend he'd probably cause this house to be attacked just like the first newspaper office and get torn to pieces by the mob. It was meant as a lighthearted gibe, but no one was laughing now.

Hall made it as far as the jail entrance when he stopped to help another man who had been knocked down. His benevolence was not rewarded. Two rioters grabbed Hall and dragged him to a corner of the lobby under a hanging light. "They held me by the wrists for about ten minutes, during which I saw several of my friends knocked down and their blood scattered over the pavement," Hall recalled. He recognized a few of the rioters from their appearance in court after the previous mob attack and assumed he'd been singled out for a "refined species of cruelty" as a result.

The mob tore off Hall's coat, rifled through his pockets and then ripped off his shirt. He tried to wriggle away, and nearly did, but he was struck on the head and crumpled to the floor. His next recollection was the sensation of a man jumping on his arm as he lay face down by the top of the front steps. After receiving several more blows, Hall was thrown down the steps and into a growing heap of bodies piled in front of the jail. There, he experienced "the most brutal and indecent outrages."

Observing through the window grates from inside his jail cell, Otho Sprigg was horrified by the scene. He watched his friends being dragged and beaten with swords and bludgeons and spotted one rioter grabbing money from the pocket of his Federalist victim. "There is not a solitary ray of compassion, or even of common humanity, to illuminate the gloom of diabolical atrocity that shrouds the behaviour of these savage ruffians," he later wrote.

The circle of rioters continued to pummel General Lingan and mock him with cries of "Tory traitor!" At one point, Lingan opened his shirt to reveal a souvenir from the Revolution—a thirty-seven-year-old purplish scar on his chest caused by a Hessian bayonet during the Battle of Fort Washington.

"Does this look as if I was a traitor?" he retorted.[48]

Lingan had paid a heavy price for his military service, but his bravery in battle against the British earned him little currency with this mob. One of the rioters reportedly threw a rock at Lingan's chest that hit him square in the spot of his wound and he again fell to the ground.

One of the last Federalists out was Major Nathaniel Musgrove. Initially, Musgrove had not attempted to escape but paced back and forth in the cell, watching and listening as his comrades fell, perhaps knowing he was only delaying the inevitable. Once his presence was discovered, he, too, was assaulted, knocked down and beaten; he was then dragged and tossed outside.

During the Revolution, James Lingan served as an officer in the Continental army and fought in the Battle of Harlem Heights in September 1776. *New York Public Library.*

Following his capture by the British in the Battle of Fort Washington, Lingan was held on HMS *Jersey*, a decommissioned ship that had been converted for storage of human cargo. Described as "a floating tomb," the *Jersey* was perhaps the most notorious of all the British prison ships, with its inhumane conditions, high incidence of infectious disease, starvation and torture. The corpses of the prisoners were usually sunk overboard in the harbor, and even many years later, local residents found skeletons washed ashore. *Library of Congress*.

"A Parcel of Hogs"

In front of the jail, eight to ten men lay in the pile, "thrown together like a parcel of hogs," according to one eyewitness. Among them were Lee and Hanson. The latter crumpled to the jail floor after an unexpected blow from Mumma and was dragged away, trampled on and finally tossed down the stairs. He had been "shockingly beaten," and some assumed he was dead. Lee was also badly beaten and in considerable pain. His mangled body lay partially on top of Hall and Hanson.

Eyewitness accounts painted a horrifying picture of the scene. "The Mob continued to torture their mangled bodies, by beating first one and then the other; sticking penknives into their faces and hands, and opening their eyes and dropping hot candle grease into them." The rioters filled one man's mouth with sand and then jammed a stick down his throat and slit his tongue.[49]

One rioter tried to cut off General Lee's nose with a knife or axe blade, but he missed and instead gave the general a bad cut on the face. Lee tried to raise his head up and saw a knife thrust toward his eye. It glanced off his cheekbone and knocked him facedown onto Hanson's chest. He lay there for several minutes, appearing nearly lifeless with blood dripping from his facial wound. When Lee's head was eventually knocked aside, the pool of blood on Hanson's torso prompted one rioter to exclaim, "See Hanson's brains on his breast!"

While the mob taunted and tortured the Federalists in front of the jail, John Thompson was being lugged into town in search of tar. When the rioters tired of dragging Thompson, they dumped him in a cart found along the way. After reaching their destination, the men ripped off Thompson's clothes and applied a coat of sticky pine tar to his head and body and then added feathers, a common form of mob violence and public humiliation. Thompson was carted around and beaten with sticks, clubs and a rusty sword. One of rioters swiped at his legs with an iron bar. Another stuck him with a pin.

"I received a few blows in my face, and very many severe bruises on different parts of my body," Thompson recalled. "My eyes were attempted to be gouged and preserved by means of the tar and feathers, though they were much injured."

Thompson, stripped nearly naked, tried to remain still and play dead to stop the attacks. The ploy might have worked, but one of the rioters decided to test the hypothesis by lighting him on fire. He lit a clump of tarred feathers with a candle and stuck it on Thompson's back. The reaction was immediate.

"I turned over suddenly, and rolled upon the flame, which put it out before it reached too great a height, but I was burnt in several parts," said Thompson. He then got to his knees and pleaded for a quick end to the torture. "For God's sake be not worse than savages: if you want my life, take it by shooting or stabbing," he said.

The rioters contemplated what to do next with their prisoner. One man wanted to hang Thompson, but others preferred to question him about Hanson and his cohorts. "If you will tell the names of all in the house and all you know about it, we will save your life," one rioter offered. Having little recourse, Thompson agreed to the deal and was carted off to a nearby tavern for questioning. [50]

Back at the jail, groans and cries of pain could be heard from the pile of bodies strewn in front of the steps. Some of the men pretended to be dead to avoid further abuse. The tactic appeared to work. One local observer later

The practice of tarring and feathering dates back at least to the twelfth century during King Richard's Crusades. The punishment was not uncommon in colonial-era America, often targeted against British Loyalists. The tar was usually a form of pine tar or resin rather than the kind of road tar we might think of today. While certainly painful to the victim, the practice was often designed more as form of vigilante justice or public humiliation. Image depicts the Whiskey Rebellion circa 1791. *New York Public Library*.

remarked that "had they not acted as Falstaff did in feigning to be dead, [it] might have been so in reality."[51]

General Lingan, however, refused to play that role. He lifted his blood-soaked head and made a plea for "permission to die in peace," according to one report. A rioter responded with a forceful blow from his club and the terse reply, "You damned old scoundrel a'nt you dead yet!"

General Lee also was badly injured, his face gashed and his right eye swollen shut and nearly blinded. He could be heard to cry out in agony, but the rioters took no pity; they mocked him as "the damned old Tory general" and claimed that even on his deathbed the general was pledging allegiance to Britain's King George. Lee did not hold back himself, calling his assailants "base villains" who disgraced the country; he remained defiant until he was rendered speechless by the blows.

In the darkened chaos, it was sometimes difficult to determine which mutilated Federalist was which amid the tangled mess. Naturally, Hanson was a particular focus of the rioters' wrath, but some of the men did not recognize him and feared he might have escaped; at one point, they took to checking the men's sleeves for initials to confirm Hanson's identity.

A few of the Federalists managed to avoid the human scrum. Daniel Murray, Hanson's brother in-law, was carried away from the jail and dumped next to the riverbank. Another Federalist named George Winchester was also separated, though neither man escaped unscathed. When he was ultimately rescued, Murray could barely walk, and he later fled to Delaware to convalesce.

The jail yard had initially erupted in bedlam after the break-in, but once the Federalist bloodletting was accomplished, a surreal tranquility eventually descended on the mob scene. It was a grayish night, and only lanterns and torches illuminated the lifeless pile of men stacked in front of the staircase. At one point, the city fire bell rang in the distance, but no militia or civil authority appeared to challenge the mob's dominion.

Having avenged the death of their leader Dr. Gale and silenced the heretical Hanson and his newspaper, the rioters paused to revel in their exploits and debate what to do with their fallen prey. Some suggested the men be buried in a hole in the ground or tossed into the Jones Falls. Castration, hanging and tarring and feathering were also offered. One rioter preferred to finish the job on the spot and simply cut all the men's throats. Another man pointed to Hanson and jabbed him with a stick in his groin. "This fellow shall be dissected!" he proclaimed.

IDENTIFYING THE RINGLEADERS

The identity of most of the individual rioters is not known. George Wolleslager, the hotheaded cordwainer, and John Mumma, the brutish butcher, both played influential roles with the mob, but there may have been as many as three hundred men present at the scene. Witnesses described the crowd as a mix of natives and immigrants, mostly Irish and some German. A few of the leading rioters can be identified based on court dockets and other eyewitness accounts. Among them were George Rodemeyer, a grocer from Fell's Point; James Darling, a local shoemaker; Edward Lathem, a chair maker; George Hayes, a hack driver; and Kenelom White, a captain in the militia. White would later take out an advertisement in the local newspaper professing his innocence, though John Hall, the attorney, specifically identified him as a leading assailant. A few of the rioters like John Gill, the militiaman who helmed the cannon, and John Maxwell, the butcher who accompanied Mumma, were property owners and slaveholders, but most came from the lower rungs of society.[52]

Hostility to Hanson's Federalists was not exclusive to one gender. A crowd of women also joined in the jail yard spectacle, egging on the rioters with taunts of their own. Described as "joyful and merry spectators," the women

BALTIMORE PRISON,
August 31st, 1812.
Capt. KENELOM WHITE having been
sent to Prison on Thursday evening, 27th
inst. by the Sheriff of Baltimore county,
between the hours of 6 and 7 o'clock—he
begs his friends and the public in general, to
suspend their opinions of his situation, until he has a trial of some kind or other. I
beg that this may be inserted in the American, the Sun, and the Whig, and likewise
the Federal Gazette. Whenever I should
have a trial, I am confident of satisfying the
public, that I am innocent of any charge of
a criminal nature
KENELOM WHITE.
sep 2   d4t

Captain Kenelom White's classified notice asked readers to "suspend their opinions" until he could prove his innocence. White, like nearly every other rioter, was later acquitted of all charges. *From the* Baltimore American and Commercial Daily Advertiser.

brooked no mercy for the fallen men. In response to pleas from the victims to spare their lives, they yelled out, "Kill the Tories." A crew of small boys also mixed with the crowd, "exulting at the awful scene, clapping their hands and skipping for joy." One local Federalist spectator recounted the massacre in a letter several days later and concluded by asking: "[A]re you not sick at the recital of this shocking affair?"[53]

To celebrate the demise of their Federalist enemies, many of the men joined hands and danced around the pile of bodies to the tune of an old Revolutionary War song. Between verses, they offered cheers to their Republican heroes Thomas Jefferson and James Madison. If they were still conscious, Lingan and Lee—the two aging military heroes who survived a war against the British only to stare down death at the hands of an American mob—might have found irony in the words of the familiar chorus:

> *We'll feather and tar ev'ry damned British tory,*
> *and that is the way for American glory.*

13

TRIAGE AND ESCAPE

They had been beaten enough to satisfy the devil.

TUESDAY LATE EVENING—It had been a whirlwind twenty-four hours, and General John Stricker was back at home with his family. After returning from the jail late in the afternoon and dismissing the militia, he retired to his parlor and left orders not to be disturbed. Stricker was exhausted from lack of sleep. His wife, who was already in a "bad state of health," had suffered anxiety and distress because of the nearby violence and the "constant and continual uproar and confusion in and about the house."

The clanging of the fire bell between eight and nine o'clock in the evening did not stir the general, nor did a visit from Sheriff Merryman, who came calling around the same time with news of the jail break-in. The sheriff was told the general was not home, though in his carefully worded deposition, Merryman later glossed over this fact and avoided placing any blame on Stricker.

Hanson's uncle John Dorsey had few such reservations. Dorsey and another unidentified Federalist also visited the general later in the evening and roused him from bed with urgent news from the jail. "Not more than one or two had been killed at the jail," Dorsey reported and opined that if the general would return with the doctors, or send guards in his place, there was still time to save the lives of others.

Stricker did not share their optimism; he doubted the mob would listen to him and assumed the Federalists were all dead by now. After the failed attempt to muster the militia earlier, he felt he had little power now to "collect men to enforce obedience to the laws." The general also shared his personal reasons for not wanting to get involved; his wife was sick, and he didn't think he should leave her. Plus, he was exhausted. "He had been up the whole of the preceding night, that he had been harassed in mind, and fatigued in body," Stricker reminded the men.

Dorsey persisted. The doctors would be able to help the fallen men if only the general or his troops would accompany them to the jail, he implored. Stricker resisted. He complained that he couldn't walk all the way to the jail in his present condition, so Dorsey offered him use of a horse. Growing impatient and out of excuses, Stricker agreed to the request. But then, just as the general walked away from the window as if to join the men, the voice of Mrs. Stricker was heard asking her husband not to leave. Her precise comments are unknown, but it was clear she'd had quite enough. A resigned Stricker returned to the window and told Dorsey "such was the situation of his family that he could not go."

RUMORS SPREAD IN THE CITY

Word of the jail attack quickly spread around the city. Early reports painted a bleak picture. Major William Barney left his house after hearing the fire bell and ran into several men rushing back from the jail. "Mr. Hanson, and his friends, were all murdered," Barney was told, "the mob had broke into the jail, had tied them together by their necks and had their brains beat out with clubs." Another apparent witness recounted that "at least eight or ten had been killed, and were laying in a heap before the jail door."

At least one report came directly from a Federalist prisoner. David Hoffman, a law school classmate of Hanson's (and future founder of the University of Maryland's School of Law) escaped from the jail relatively unscathed and made his way to the home of a friend in Old Town. He described the awful scene of bodies in front of the jail, believing that most of his friends were dead.

Even Sheriff Merryman assumed the worst. After his fruitless attempt to find help in town, Merryman returned to the jail yard with one of his officers. "We witnessed a sight shocking to humanity," he recalled after seeing the rioters and the pile of bodies near the steps. Realizing the futility of further action, and perhaps sensing that his own safety was tenuous, Merryman fled the scene.

He was not alone. Several witnesses described similar reactions. "When I reached the jail, they were throwing the dead bodies in a heap, a few steps from the jail door," one local merchant recalled. He started turning over bodies, looking for a friend, but was quickly grabbed by the coat and warned to leave immediately. "I took his advice, and left this scene of blood and horror," the man said.

William Gwynn was also shaken at the sight of his friends stacked in front of jail, calling it "too distressing, too horrible to witness." After his failed attempt to aid General Lingan, Gwynn decided to leave, fearing that "any further exertions would not only be unavailing, but would also subject me to imminent danger."

A Doctor Saves the Day

While most of Baltimore's leading residents fretted from afar or fled the scene in fear, an unlikely savior stepped forward. Dr. Richard W. Hall had a medical degree from the University of Pennsylvania and served as attending physician for the penitentiary. Dr. Hall was a Republican from a prominent Maryland family, but unlike the slain mob leader Dr. Gale, his medical bona fides were never in question.

When Dr. Hall arrived, many of the rioters were still gathered around the pile of Federalists and reveling in song. He introduced himself to their apparent leader, Captain Kenelom White, and expressed shock at the spectacle. "He said he was as much of a Republican as any of them—but his Republicanism could not approve of such proceedings," recalled John Hall (no known relation). Thinking quickly, Dr. Hall informed the rioters that none of the Federalists was likely to recover and most were probably dead already. Accordingly, he suggested the bodies be delivered back into the jail cell under his care so that he could later use them as cadavers for medical research. Physicians were always looking for bodies to dissect, and these Federalists might offer some "very good Tory skeletons," he said.

Dr. Hall's proposal was readily accepted. The mob had yet to reach a consensus on what to do with the prisoners, and this suggestion made as much sense as any other. Moreover, the prospect of the Federalists being dissected may have pleased some of the bloodthirsty rioters. With help from the mob, Dr. Hall and several of his medical colleagues started carrying the bodies back up the stairs into the jail cell.

While the doctors were attending to the prisoners, John Thompson was still living his own nightmare. After being tarred, feathered, burned and generally "beaten to a mummy," Thompson was taken by cart to the Bull's Horse Tavern in Fell's Point by a dozen or so rioters. He was weak from the loss of blood and eagerly drank several shots of whiskey. According to one report, the mob also held a flaming candle under his nose to stir him. The men detained him for about an hour and demanded to know the names of all the Federalists in the house and everything he knew about Hanson's plan. There was little new information to be gleaned, and Thompson was in no condition to put up a fight, so he divulged what he knew.

When they were done, the rioters decided to bring him to the watch house for the night so he could repeat his confession to the magistrate the next morning. In his weakened condition, Thompson had trouble walking and stopped several times to rest. Some of the rioters grew impatient at his pace and suggested that since he'd already divulged the information they ought to just hang him now. One man warned Thompson they "would cut off [his] head and stick it on a pole." An informal poll was taken among the rioters, with a majority voting in favor of hanging Thompson. But before the sentence could be carried out, the men were reminded of the deal they'd struck: Thompson had lived up to his end of the bargain, plus he might still provide useful information. Calmer heads prevailed, and the mob delivered Thompson to the watch house later in the evening.

Once the Federalist bodies had been dragged back into the jail, the doctors examined their wounds. The jail cell was soon transformed into an impromptu emergency room. It was tight quarters, and keeping the men from rolling over onto one another was a concern. Those who were conscious were offered spirits and opiates. Some of the rioters stuck around the jail cell watching the scene—or, as one Federalist described it, "glutting their cannibal appetites with the sight of our wounds, and the sound of our groans."

In addition to Dr. Hall, several other local doctors helped treat the Federalists. One physician active in assisting was Dr. James Page, who went by the nickname "Boston Beauty" for unknown reasons. Another was Dr. John Owen, a fellow Republican, who rushed up to the jail after learning about the break-in. It wasn't his first encounter with the mob. Dr. Owen was present during the first mob riot in June and helped prevent an attack on the bank.

"I instantly rode to the jail, when I found nine persons dreadfully cut and bruised, most of them senseless," Dr. Owen recalled.

After triaging the men's injuries as best they could, some of the doctors left the jail to find carriages to transport the wounded. It was late into the night, and the mob scene outside the jail had quieted. Whether they were merely fatigued, or, in the words of one Federalist, "satiated with the cruelties already committed," some rioters departed after the prisoners were carted inside. Mumma the butcher remained, as did Wolleslager and others. The remaining mob allowed the physicians to bring medical supplies into the jail but refused to allow any of the Federalists to leave.

Hanson doubted the mob would let him live through to the morning if he stayed in the jail. He asked the doctors to help him escape and get to his brother-in-law's house, where his family was staying, about three miles outside the city. He was right to be worried; the mob's fury had not subsided. Hanson had suffered numerous head wounds, an "inflammation of the brain," a spinal injury, a broken nose and fingers and possibly a broken collarbone. His right hand was stabbed twice with a penknife, once clean through. Still, the mob's ringleaders were not satisfied and "spoke with indignation of his having suffered less than others." They reiterated their desire to kill Hanson in the morning and then tar and feather any other Federalists who survived the night.

Dr. Owen asked Bentley the jailer for help. Would he help extricate Hanson and the other Federalists safely from of the jail? Initially, Bentley objected; the prisoners were still in his custody, he said, and he could not just let them go. Hanson interjected, reminding the jailer that his duty was extinguished once the mob had broken in.

"Very well, do as you please," the jailer replied.

Bentley agreed to consult with the sheriff and ask for the Federalists' release. He and another man left the jail and headed into town. It was close to two o'clock in the morning when they knocked at the sheriff's door and awoke him from his slumber. Sheriff Merryman had left the jail much earlier under the assumption all the prisoners were dead. After a brief conversation, the trio headed off to the home of Judge Scott to request an official release.

Hanson had little faith in the civil authority and wasn't eager to wait for permission. Soon after Bentley's departure, he and Dr. Owen decided it was too risky to delay any longer. The ranks of the mob had thinned, and some of the men were preoccupied in the jailer's office. This was their opportunity to make a break for it, but there was one problem: Hanson was in no condition to be moved. He tried to stand up and promptly fell down, fainting each time he tried to rise. The doctors gave him a glass of spirits, either brandy or rum, and Hanson "was quickly invigorated."

Under the aid of Dr. Owen and another man, Hanson was able to stand and exit the cell. John Hall and Harry Nelson also decided to leave and followed Hanson out. The other Federalists remained. Some were too injured to move on their own, including General Lee and Major Musgrove.

FAREWELL TO GENERAL LINGAN

Before departing, Hanson lingered over the motionless figure of General Lingan, who had earlier pronounced to his friend that "he could not die in a better cause." Lingan's blood-caked head was gashed in several places, his skull likely fractured. Lingan's shirt was ripped apart, revealing the bayonet scar on his chest from the Revolutionary War. After the beatings, he was carried back inside the jail with the rest of the Federalists. Soon after, he drew his last breath.

One witness later described Lingan's final words as he reached his hand out to a fellow Federalist: "Farewell, I am a dying man, make your escape, return home and take care there—"[54]

The words trailed off, and the celebrated war hero succumbed to his injuries. Lingan thus became the mob's first victim, one of the earliest casualties of the War of 1812 and the first documented death in defense of the free press in the young nation's history.[55]

HANSON MAKES HIS ESCAPE

Hanson had little time to reflect on the significance of the moment. His own life was still in jeopardy. Dr. Owen and another man named Griffin hurried him off and headed to the outer jail door. One of the men carried Hanson on his back, and in the darkness, they scurried out the exit and over to the nearby Jones Falls, directly west of the jail, while John Hall and Harry Nelson followed behind. Here the men split up. Dr. Owen stopped to distract a group of five or six mob members who approached, while Griffin took Hanson across the stream and found him a hiding spot in a small garden on the opposite bank. Hall did not have the strength to cross and hid in a dark gulley. Nelson found shelter in a cart covered by hay.

The small group of rioters angrily questioned Dr. Owen about Hanson and searched the area. They did not find any trace of the Federalists but "repeated with great violence their former threats to me," Dr. Owen recalled. He then returned to the jail to attend to the other prisoners. When he felt the way was clear, Hanson crawled away to safety and later met up with Nelson. Hall hid out much of the night and eventually found shelter at the home of a "humane gentleman" who lived nearby.

When he returned to the jail, Dr. Owen and the other physicians worked to arrange medical care for the remaining prisoners. Their efforts were aided by the return of Sheriff Merryman, accompanied by Dr. James Smith and an official release signed by the judge. While the sheriff consulted with Mumma, Wolleslager and the other mob ringleaders, the physicians used the opportunity to sneak three more prisoners out of the jail by hiding them in a carriage that was supposed to carry the doctors back into town. Dr. Peregrine Warfield, Charles J. Kilgour and William Gaither were brought to a nearby mill and then to the home of Warfield's father for medical care.

General Lee and Major Musgrove remained in the jail, as did General Lingan, whose body was now covered by a sheet. After some convincing, most of the remaining rioters grudgingly agreed to allow the remaining Federalists to get medical care. John Mumma, the butcher who had led the massacre, even helped convince a few stubborn holdouts. "They had been beaten enough to satisfy the devil," he told Dr. Owen.

Mumma helped the doctors sew General Lee's nose back on and aided in carrying the men out on blankets and into a carriage. A pair of rioters then accompanied Dr. Owen to deliver the patients to the hospital. Despite this change in attitude, the mob's enmity toward the Federalists remained. "While in the room with them, sarcastical and abusive remarks were made about [the Federalists'] foreign dress, Virginia boots, Montgomery coats," Dr. Owen recalled. It served as a reminder that the rioters' hostility was built on class resentment as well as political division.

By sunrise on Wednesday, the Federalists had been delivered to the hospital, which was located due east of the jail on the outskirts of the city center. John Thompson, who had spent the night in the watch house after being beaten nearly to death, was escorted in later in the morning by the mayor. Thompson was put in a room next to Lee and could hear his groans, evidence that the general was not dead, as many initially believed.

One local Federalist visited the men at the hospital and later described their condition: "Lee was as black as a negro, his head cut to pieces without a hat…or any shirt but a flannel one which was covered with blood. One eye

Some of the injured Federalists were brought to the Baltimore hospital located east of the jail. J.H. Latrobe. *Johns Hopkins University.*

apparently out, his clothes torn and covered with blood from tip to toe, and when he attempted to stir he tottered like an infant just commencing to walk. Thompson [was] equally abused and disgusting."[56]

As soon as the men were stable enough, efforts were made to move them. While the hospital could tend to their wounds, it was not necessarily a place of safety for the Federalists. The mob had broken into a jail after all—coming after them in a hospital would be much easier. The city remained in a state of emergency; even the local courthouse was shut down on Wednesday morning out of safety concerns. Friends arranged for a carriage to bring General Lee and Thompson into the country and deliver them to safe hands across the state line in York, Pennsylvania.

Thompson described his condition a few days later in words that many of his fellow Federalist victims would probably share: "I cherish the hope, that I shall survive all the bruises and wounds, which have been so cruelly and maliciously inflicted by a wicked and lawless Mob, and that I shall be again restored to the full use and enjoyment of my bodily powers."

14

MAKINGS OF MOBTOWN

*The devoted city of Baltimore is completely given up to the domination of a mob
more savage and inhuman than the ruffians of the French revolution.*
—Frederick-Town Herald, *August 1, 1812*

WEDNESDAY—The chaos of Tuesday night soon turned to paralysis. Much of Baltimore awoke on a hot Wednesday morning to news of the riot at the jail and the massacre of the Federalists. City business came to a halt, markets closed and trade ceased. Many residents hunkered down, and some skittish Federalists fled the city. Federalist supporters who remained "spoke with caution and in whispers, lest they should be overheard." The criminal court opened its regular Wednesday session and promptly adjourned to the following week, with the grand jury reportedly declaring, "The Peace of the City was violated and all Laws being at an end."[57]

A few brave curiosity seekers ventured up to the jail on Wednesday to survey the carnage. Among them was William Barney, the cavalry major, who was curious how the jail door had been breached and rode up at first light to investigate. He found the rear door and turned a key in the lock: it clicked and the door opened easily. Other than a damaged hasp, the lock was in working order. Barney's suspicion was thus confirmed—the door had been opened from the inside, and the jailer must be to blame.

"I felt myself wound up to a pitch," he recalled.

Inside the jail, Barney saw evidence of the massacre everywhere: blood smears and tattered clothing, red handprints on the wall, a soiled hat showing evidence of a blow. He found a black coat in the corner with its sleeves turned inside out caked with blood. In one pocket was a red bandana, in the other a folded copy of the *Federal Republican* and a necktie with the initials H.N., probably belonging to Hanson's friend Harry Nelson.

Another witness at the jail on Wednesday morning reported seeing a man he suspected was Mumma holding a sheet over the corpse of General Lingan, whose body was lying on the floor. All the other Federalists had been carried off or managed to escape, but no one had yet figured out what to do with Lingan's body. "Look at the damn'd old Tory general," Mumma reportedly said. The witness found the callous remarks "shocking to the feelings of humanity."

CITY LEADERS FACE FIRE

Later that day, Mayor Johnson convened an emergency meeting in the council chamber. He knew that recriminations would soon be brewing and may have been eager to engage in damage control. Johnson met with some of his supporters earlier in the day and offered to resign his office, but they urged him not to. The public meeting would present a more challenging audience. Many of the city's leading residents attended, including a few Federalists like William Gwynn.

Before the meeting, Gwynn bumped into the mayor at the bottom of the stairs leading to the council chamber. "I spoke to him of the distressing scenes of the preceding night," Gwynn recalled. He found the mayor still in an emotional state and disturbed by the night's events.

"If it was distressing to you what must it have been to me, who had pledged my honor to those men to protect them at the risk of my life?" the mayor asked. He admitted that his plan to convince the mob to stand down using peaceful persuasion was a mistake.

Gywnn told Johnson he believed many citizens had left the jail and were dissuaded from lending aid because of an erroneous report circulating around the city that there was no danger to the Federalists that night. The mayor expressed his surprise and asked who reported such a rumor.

Attorney General John Montgomery happened to be walking up the stairs at the time, and Gwynn identified him as one. The mayor turned and questioned Montgomery. "My God, Sir, how could you circulate such a report, when it must have been obvious to any person who was near the

Attorney William Gwynn shared Hanson's Federalist sentiments but not his fiery temperament. When Gwynn later took reins of another Federalist newspaper in Baltimore, he wrote of his goal to "unite moderation with firmness." Gwynn was once described as "one of the kindest and most benevolent of men, loved by all who knew him." *Baltimore Bar Library Collection.*

jail, and heard the discourse and threats of the people, that there was the greatest danger?"

Montgomery didn't deny circulating the report but claimed that he was merely the messenger; the firsthand information had come from General Stricker.

Stricker was also present at the meeting, and when it was over, he approached Gwynn. He knew he was being blamed for dismissing the militia and launched into a lengthy explanation for his actions. He had ordered out the Fifth Regiment, a pair of artillery companies and two cavalry troops, but only a fraction reported for duty, he explained. Many of those were Federalists, a fact that would not sit well with the mob, since it was composed primarily of Republicans, and he feared they could inflame the passions rather than douse them.

The council chamber meeting wrapped up after a heated discussion on the best way to preserve peace in the city. Some residents wanted to form a posse comitatus to patrol the streets, while others felt the threat had largely receded now that "the cause which had produced them was removed." No consensus was reached, and a further gathering was planned for the mayor's house around eight o'clock Wednesday evening.

During the evening meeting, an ad hoc citizen's group formed with a charge to investigate the riots and report back to the mayor on the best means to "quiet the apprehensions of the people, and restore peace and tranquility." Among them were William Gwynn, General Stricker, Lemuel Taylor and John Montgomery. This citizen's group decided a more formal inquiry was required and asked the mayor to call in a special session of both branches of the city council.

A "DANGEROUS SPIRIT"

The week ended without further mob incidents reported, though the city remained in a state of emergency and tensions ran high. The mob, factious and fractured, congregated in smaller groups in various parts of the city, including a neighborhood meeting called on Friday night at Pamphilion's Hotel in Fell's Point.[58]

William Gwynn, a respected voice in the city, lamented what he saw as the rapid descent into partisan vitriol in the immediate aftermath of the riots. Public reaction within the city was forming through a binary lens, he wrote, one that ascribed blame, or praise, depending on which side one was on. "This dangerous spirit was rapidly changing party opposition into personal animosity," he said.

Gwynn later described a conversation with another well-known resident, Levi Hollingsworth, shortly after the jail attack. Hollingsworth, a Republican, felt that Hanson and his newspaper had purposefully provoked the mob attack and deserved their fate.

"The editors of that paper, and all their supporters, were traitors," Hollingsworth said. "The men who defended the house in Charles Street had been guilty of a violent outrage in first provoking the people to attack them, and then firing on them."

Gwynn countered by asking whether Hollingsworth thought it proper for the mob to serve as judge and executioner even if the Federalists were guilty of provoking the attack.

Hollingsworth gestured in the direction of the courthouse and spoke disparagingly of the uncertainty and delays in dispensing justice. "No, I am for having immediate justice on them. The people ought to have put them to death on the spot," he told Gwynn, who found the same alarming sentiment shared among other prominent residents as well.

Hanson himself, still recuperating from his injuries outside the city, feared the same mob mentality seeping into the public consciousness. "If they look on quietly…and permit a hundreth [*sic*] part of the population of any place…to usurp the government, they may blame themselves when *their* property, persons and families are disposed of by the same rules of 'summary adjudication,'" he wrote.[59]

NEWS SPREADS OUTSIDE OF BALTIMORE

While Baltimore was still reeling from the turmoil, news of the mob attacks began spreading outside the city. Many of the early accounts came in the form of letters and reports passed along by stagecoach, though not all of the details were accurate. A Philadelphia newspaper reported on Thursday that General Lee, Hanson and John Thompson had all been killed. The next day, it updated readers with news that Hanson and Thompson had survived and Lee was still alive, "though still little hope was entertained of his recovery."[60]

The various reports prompted strong reactions. One of Hanson's political heroes, Timothy Pickering, a Federalist from Massachusetts, shared his joy upon learning initial reports of Hanson's death were incorrect. "No death since that of [Alexander] Hamilton excited so much regret. I viewed him as one of the brilliant lights and distinguished heroes of his country, destined to guide and save it. God be praised that this hope and expectation are not extinguished," Pickering wrote.[61]

Attempts to spin the facts in the press to deflect blame or achieve political gain also began almost immediately. The *Baltimore Whig* jumped on the story on Wednesday "to prevent the false statements from the Tory faction" and cast blame on the Federalists—referred to as "Montgomery conspirators" to emphasize they were not from Baltimore—for instigating the attacks. General Lee was referred to as "the swindling Harry Lee," a jab at his failed foray into land speculation; Hanson's *Federal Republican* was assailed for "breathing its accustomed spirit of treason."

The *National Intelligencer*, a leading Republican-leaning newspaper in Washington, was more measured in tone. It published an article on Saturday regarding the "Dreadful Commotion" and urged readers not to

BALTIMORE MOB!!

To destroy the Freedom of Speech, and of the Press.

Horrid OUTRAGES—and Savage MURDERS—

AT BALTIMORE!

Constitutionalist Office, (Monday Evening) August 3, 1812.

From a Handbill this moment arrived in town, we learn the following heart-rending particulars. We are almost struck dumb with horror and dismay, when we reflect on the disasterous consequences of of a CIVIL WAR, begun on the part of the *Friends of Administration*, in the only democratic seaport on the continent.— All this and more are we to expect from harbouring lawless Frenchmen in the bosom of our country—Oh! Liberty! Oh! New-England! unite if you have any hopes of political salvation.

From a Philadelphia Paper.

On Monday morning last between 12 and 1 o'clock, another mob assembled at the Office of the *Federal Republican*, No. 45, S. Charles-Street, for the purpose of demolishing it and committing violence on Alexander C. Hanson, Esq. one of the Editors.— As the papers published in that City are silent on the subject, we are obliged to depend on letters for particulars.

given up to the mob. Mr. Wagner was at Georgetown.

The mail is about to close—the mob is very numerous and active at this moment—the mayor will do nothing— The military acted without command or officers—The Lord have mercy upon us. It is impossible to know how many are killed or wounded.

FURTHER.

By the stage last evening from Baltimore we have received the following account of a most horrible outrage;

The mob which had collected in front of the jail to the number of 2000, or thereabouts, procured a field piece, and about 11 at night broke into the jail where they killed 12 of the defenceless persons who had been placed there by the civil authority. Among the killed, we are told are a Gen. Harry Lee, Mr. Hanson and a Mr. Thompson, whose bodies, horrible to relate, were tarred and feathered and carried thro' town in savage triumph.—The names of the others who were killed we have not heard. A Mr. Bigelow, and sev-

seize again upon the others who were beaten, but survived, and who are now in the Hospital and not expected to live until 12 o'clock. I am sorry to have to mention it as a fact that the criminal court which was in session have adjourned to avoid interfering.

Further Particulars.

Baltimore, July 29, 1812.

We have had another dreadful night. You have learned that Mr. Hanson, and some 25 or 26 of his friends had capitulated with the Mayor and Gen. Striker, to surrender themselves to the civil authority, and at their own request were committed to jail, their safety from the mob being guaranteed by the General and Mayor. The troops were ordered out for the protection of the prison, and to keep the peace of the city; but, to their eternal disgrace, they refused to obey. About 9 o'clock the mob forced the jail, and fell with the fury of cannibals, on the 26 unarmed prisoners, and assaulted them with bludgeons until no signs of life remained, when they left them.

In Federalist New England, where antiwar sentiment ran strong, the propaganda machine was quick to capitalize. A two-page handbill distributed in Boston blasted out news of the attacks. *Massachusetts Historical Society.*

be "assailed by rumors" and exaggerations. The newspaper pointed out that the Federalists defending the house on Charles Street were heavily armed and speculated that the "garrisoning of an armed citadel in the midst of their city" might have sparked the mob's anger. By the weekend, newspapers up the East Coast had jumped on the theme. One New York daily predicted that Federalists would use the riots to "expatiate with crocodile tears against *mob law*" but fail to acknowledge the incendiary words of Hanson and his "rebellious friends in arms."[62]

The press and the public clamored for a full accounting of the riots, and on Monday, the Baltimore City Council attempted to do this. The two branches met and approved a plan presented by Mayor Johnson to launch a formal investigation. A joint committee was appointed, comprising the president and three members from each branch along with thirteen citizens at large (though only ten signed the final report), with orders to report back in three days.

The committee boasted participation of "citizens of all political parties," but it was dominated by Republicans. Of the sixteen members selected, at least eleven were Republicans while two were Federalists, including William Gwynn. The party affiliation of the remaining members is unknown. A sum of $500 was later appropriated for the effort. Operating under a short deadline and without the ability to take testimony under oath, the tribunal nonetheless "seemed to produce reflection and to arrest violence, and men came forward who were not before to be seen," according to one participant.

NEWSPAPER REVIVED IN GEORGETOWN

While the committee investigation progressed, another development threw a wrench into the works. A new edition of the *Federal Republican*, issued from Georgetown, arrived at the Baltimore post office on Tuesday. At Hanson's urging, his partner Jacob Wagner published the latest edition, which featured a lengthy report on the latest mob attacks, outlined in black for effect:

> *THE MASSACRE AT BALTIMORE—The history of barbarians scarcely affords a parallel in perfidy and cruelty to the late transactions at Baltimore...*

In more than two thousand words, the paper recounted the events leading up to the Charles Street attack and the subsequent break-in at the jail, the brutal beatings and the death of Lingan. Mayor Johnson and General Stricker were again singled out for criticism, though blame went to wide swaths of Baltimore city leadership. The report also mocked attempts in the Republican press to portray Hanson as the provoker:

> *Justice here is completely reversed, massacre is lawful, self-defense is treason, the innocent and injured party threatened with punishment, and the most enormous criminals sanction by our government writers.*

A postscript to the account shared an excerpt from a letter written by Hanson to Wagner that had been penned three days earlier, one of the first he had written since the attack. In it, Hanson urged his partner to resume publication of the *Federal Republican* with "accustomed vigor." It's not clear if Hanson actually wrote the letter or dictated it to someone else. In another letter posted the same day, Hanson revealed that his doctors advised him not to write or talk due to the severity of his injuries. Despite the ordeal, he remained defiant and dedicated to the principle of a free press. "My wounds are many and bad but my spirits are unbroken and my determination to have justice unaltered," he wrote.[63]

MOB MOVES AGAINST POST OFFICE

This new issue of the *Federal Republican* was delivered to the Baltimore post office and immediately caused a stir. Postmaster Charles Burrall, a respected Federalist who had served in the position for nearly a dozen years, suspected another attack might be in the works when a large number of individuals who did not appear to be subscribers began inquiring about the paper. He left to track down the mayor and eventually found him in a meeting with General Stricker, Lemuel Taylor and several others. Initially, the men were skeptical that the post office was in any real danger, but Burrall convinced them the threat was real and Stricker issued orders to call out the militia again.

Later that evening—precisely one week after the riot at the jail—the Baltimore mob struck again, though this time the city was better prepared. Militia troops were posted along the street at each intersection near the post office. They included cavalry troops from Fell's Point under the command of Lieutenant Colonel James Biays as well as several other cavalry companies and Colonel Joseph Sterett's infantry. Mindful of the criticism he was still subjected to for leaving the jail the previous week, this time, General Stricker remained on the scene (though in civilian clothes) joined by Attorney General John Montgomery. The mayor was also conspicuously present, mounted on horseback and wielding a sword.

The mob of men collected on the street and in front of the building included George Wolleslager, the hot-tempered cordwainer who had led the attack on the jail. One man had a large bludgeon. "They were very noisy, and swore they would have the *Federal Republican* out of the [post] office," a witness recalled.

Many of the militia members were not pleased once they realized they had been called out to protect the *Federal Republican* newspaper and not just the post office. Major William Barney approached the mayor and warned him of the impending mutiny. After several discussions, the mayor dismounted and met with a small group of men from one of the militia companies in a nearby bank. They were angry and mistrustful.

"Mr. Johnson you have deceived us, if we had known that you were bringing us here to defend the *Federal Republican* not a man of us would have turned out," one of the men said.

"My friends you are mistaken, I brought you here to defend the laws and constitution of our country," the mayor replied, "and do not carry your prejudices against the *Federal Republican* so far as to suffer the post office to come down."

The mayor departed angrily and returned to General Stricker and Colonel Sterett, reporting his fears that the militia would soon abandon them. The men decided to notify the postmaster what was happening.

"Mr. Burrall, we are of opinion that your office cannot be defended," the mayor announced and suggested the newspapers be removed to a safer location and then returned to Georgetown in the morning. Burrall insisted the post office must be defended and that he would not give up the newspapers, as it would violate his oath as postmaster and subject him to disqualification or sanction.

The mayor remained unconvinced. He did not believe the post office, or any other building in the city, could be defended so long as it housed the *Federal Republican*. Under the circumstances, he felt they would be justified in returning the newspapers to the sender, but Burrall disagreed. He said he did not have the authority to return the newspapers. Not even the president of the United States could take such action, he said. "Nothing but an act of Congress could deprive [the Federalists] of their rights in the mail."

The conversation was occurring in front of the post office within earshot of the mob, so Burrall suggested they adjourn to the parlor in his home, located nearby on St. Paul's Lane. General Stricker and Lemuel Taylor joined them, and Burrall bolted the door behind them for privacy. He reiterated his reasons for defending the newspaper and eventually overcame the opposition.

"You are right, by God your office must and shall be defended, and sir, I pledge myself to you that it shall be defended," Lemuel Taylor promised. Stricker and the mayor ultimately concurred.

The mayor emerged, newly emboldened, and addressed the crowd gathered in front of the post office. He ordered "all good and peaceable citizens" to stand down and said the mob had "ruled the city long enough."

TRENTON FEDERALIST.

MONDAY, AUGUST 3, 1812.

Mobs, Butchery and Murder.

The most distressing intelligence from Mob-Town (formerly Baltimore) has continued to agitate the public most part of the past week.

The publication of the *Federal Republican*, the Printing office of which was destroyed by the mob, a few weeks ago, was resumed at George-town, and the paper issued from the distributing office at Baltimore on Monday last. The evening following the refuse population of that abandoned place, was assembled through the instigation of their wicked leaders for the purpose committing fresh outrages. The mayor was informed of the expected riot, but instead of taking measures

This New Jersey newspaper published one of earliest known references to "Mob Town" on August 3, 1812. *From the* Trenton Federalist.

General Stricker informed one of the militia field officers that his men were free to leave if they were not willing to fulfill their duties, but only one man accepted the offer. Biays followed up with an order to disperse the crowd and drew his sword. A handful of his cavalry charged at the mob, and the rabble retreated. A few skirmishes were reported throughout the evening, but the militia held the mob in check and the post office and the newspapers inside were protected.

Late Tuesday night, the mob withdrew, and the building was not breached. For the next several evenings, the militia was called out in force to protect the post office and quell any disturbances in the city. An artillery piece was also set up nearby in case it was needed to repel an attack. The postmaster applauded the efforts of the militia, as well as Mayor Johnson and General Stricker, who "persevered with great zeal and patience." The mayor was also pleased with the response and later boasted of the steps taken since the jail attack. "The military were called upon daily and always obeyed. The ringleaders were indicted by the Grand Jury, apprehended, and committed to prison," he recalled.

City leaders had reacted with far more urgency to defend the post office than they had the Federalists in the jail, and the streets of Baltimore soon regained a temporary peace. But even before this latest incident, the shockwaves were rippling in and outside the city. One Federalist writing to a family member right after the attack made an ominous prediction: "The consequences of this dreadful business will have a lasting and unfortunate effect on Baltimore."[64]

The long-term impact was to be determined, but one result was already known: Baltimore had earned a sobering new nickname, "Mobtown."[65]

INVESTIGATIONS AND RECRIMINATIONS

Mobs however must be prevented, & the punishment even of such men as the Editors of that paper must be inflicted by law, not mob movements.

NEAR BALTIMORE, C. AUGUST 1, 1812—Alexander Hanson spent the first days after the attack recuperating near Baltimore and later returned to his home in Rockville accompanied by a pair of "fellow sufferers" in Harry Nelson and Charles Kilgore. He felt safer in Montgomery County but was still concerned enough about his safety to consider posting a guard or leaving the state altogether.

Hanson was initially well enough to go out riding but soon suffered a relapse and remained under the care of a doctor, mostly confined to bed. "For the last five days I…can now bare raise my head high enough to direct my pen. The wounds on my head have broke out afresh and I am so debilitated by the loss of blood," he wrote.[66]

Despite his injuries, Hanson emerged from the attack in better shape than General Lee. After leaving the hospital in Baltimore, Lee was shipped to York, Pennsylvania, where it was believed he would be safer. Early on, his friends feared he would not survive, and a number of newspapers actually reported his death. It was only a slight exaggeration: the massacre had rendered him nearly comatose.

"He cannot yet converse or take any other sustenance except liquids, and of those very little," one witness said. "He…is able to make himself understood by uttering a word or two at a time and making signs." The account, published in local newspapers, also contained a lengthy description of Lee's injuries by his doctors:

> On his left cheek there is a deep cut as if made with a penknife, his nose was slit open with a knife as far as the bridge, and having been immediately sewed up, seems to be united and is doing well and the nose has it's [sic] natural form. His right eye has been dreadfully bruised, and is still closed....He sees out of the left eye, which also was severely bruised, and both sides of his head, his whole face and his throat from his ears to the breast bone are shockingly bruised and much swollen.

Once his life appeared to be out of danger, plans were made to bring Lee to his home in Alexandria. On the way, he stopped in to visit with Hanson at his home in Rockville. Hanson was happy to see his friend but saddened by the depth of his apparent suffering. "It was agonizing to behold the features of such a man, distorted by wounds inflicted on him by a savage mob," the *Federal Republican* wrote.

Lee's disfiguring wounds attracted attention, even at his church in Alexandria. A ten-year-old girl who wrote her memoirs many years later recalled looking over and seeing the general sitting in his pew at church with his children, including a young Robert E. Lee. She was startled by the elder Lee's appearance.

"His bright penetrating look was made a terror to me and other children because the bright black eyes were shining under white bandages that bound his brow, and others passing over his head and under his chin," she wrote. "We were told that he had been a great warrior in the revolt from England, but that the wounds under the bandages had been inflicted in Baltimore where he was defending the press and printing office from the violence of a lawless mob."[67]

INVESTIGATION BEGINS IN BALTIMORE

Back in Baltimore, city leaders were attempting to restore order. A curfew of eight o'clock was established, and the militia remained on call. The city investigation into the riots continued, and on Thursday, August 6, the two branches of the Baltimore City Council met and unanimously approved a report investigating "the late commotions in the city." It was a "sultry day" with "some thunder but no rain, more cool in the evening."[68]

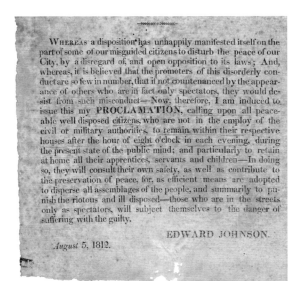

WHEREAS a disposition has unhappily manifested itself on the part of some of our misguided citizens to disturb the peace of our City, by a disregard of, and open opposition to its laws; And, whereas, it is believed that the promoters of this disorderly conduct are so few in number, that if not countenanced by the appearance of others who are in fact only spectators, they would desist from such misconduct—Now, therefore, I am induced to issue this my **PROCLAMATION**, calling upon all peaceable well disposed citizens, who are not in the employ of the civil or military authorities, to remain within their respective houses after the hour of eight o'clock in each evening, during the present state of the public mind; and particularly to retain at home all their apprentices, servants and children—In doing so, they will consult their own safety, as well as contribute to the preservation of peace, for, as efficient means are adopted to disperse all assemblages of the people, and summarily to punish the riotous and ill disposed—those who are in the streets only as spectators, will subject themselves to the danger of suffering with the guilty.

EDWARD JOHNSON.

August 5, 1812.

Mayor Johnson instituted a city curfew of eight o'clock in an attempt to prevent "misguided citizens" from disturbing the peace. *Duke University Library.*

News of the mob attacks had already spread in newspapers and letters, but most of the accounts were brief dispatches, opinions or rumors, often shared by travelers. The city's investigation was the first attempt to set out a comprehensive account of the rioting. In about 1,250 words, the report described the events leading up to the massacre, including the publication of the first editorial in the *Federal Republican* ("which excited great irritation in the city") and the lengthy siege of the house on Charles Street. Dr. Gale's death was recounted, but details about his murder were left ambiguous. The report candidly acknowledged the brutal attack at the jail ("here a scene of horror ensued which the committee cannot well describe") but was careful not to blame city officials.

After approving the release of the joint report and ordering publication in local newspapers, the council met again the next day and issued a public statement of its own that emphasized that the report was not merely a Republican effort but one that included participation from "respectable citizens of all political parties."

> *Can you read it without the most awful sensations? Can you look back without horror upon the fatal events of the 27th and 28th of July?... Citizens of Baltimore, public tranquility is again restored, and we exhort you to maintain it....Civil and political liberty can only be maintained by an obedience to the laws and respect of the civil authority.*

The report was accompanied by several letters addressed to Hanson and his colleagues prior to their return to Baltimore. Some detailed preparations made by the Federalists for the house on Charles Street, including recommendations about what weapons and munitions to bring. "Lathing hatchets may be a good substitute for tomahawks if they cannot be had," a man named Colonel John Lynn advised in a letter to Hanson's cousin. The existence of the letters was generally known thanks to the *Baltimore Whig*, which circulated them in an attempt to embarrass Hanson by showing that he arrived in the city well armed. The fact that the letters were included in the city council report rankled some committee members, though others believed it was "the least evil" to include them, in part to dispel rumors around the city that greatly exaggerated their contents.

The joint report and the accompanying letters were widely disseminated in the press in Maryland and along the East Coast. Reaction came swiftly. John Hall was still recuperating from his injuries in Philadelphia when he read the report. He and two other Federalists immediately issued a statement of their own challenging the city council's version of events and making "a request to the public that no definite judgment may be formed from a statement which is utterly untrue in the most important particulars."

Other Federalists were eager to get their story into the public domain. John Thompson, still recuperating from his tarring and feathering, wrote a detailed account of his ordeal that was published the same week. Hall himself followed up later in the month with a lengthy statement given under oath and first published in a Philadelphia newspaper. Otho Sprigg, who had witnessed the massacre of his friends from the opposing jail cell, gave a sworn statement in Fredericksburg, Maryland.

Despite the blows to his head, Hanson's political instincts remained sharp, and he urged his colleagues to get their own narratives on the record. The group met before a justice of the peace in Montgomery County on August 12. They included Hanson, John Payne, Richard Crabb, Henry Gaither, Ephraim Gaither, Robert Kilgour, Charles Kilgour, Harry Nelson and Peregrine Warfield. Their statement, titled "An Exact and Authentic Narrative," described the authors as "some of the surviving persons who were devoted...to the brutal and murderous fury of the Mob, in the late Massacre in the Jail." In more than nine thousand words, it offered a richly detailed, though one-sided, report of the entire ordeal from the original mob attack in June up through the jail massacre and escape.

As a postscript to their own reporting of events, the Federalists offered a rebuttal to the Baltimore city council report, which they read with "mingled regret and indignation." The fact that some respected citizens had signed on to the committee report rankled them in particular, probably a reference to William Gwynn. The Federalists also used the opportunity to defend themselves against insinuations that they had conspired to provoke the mob attacks:

> *Understanding that the justification made for the barbarous cruelties which treachery and black malignity procured to be inflicted upon them, is that an extensive conspiracy was formed to murder, or otherwise molest the citizens of Baltimore, the above named do, therefore, solemnly swear that no such conspiracy or association ever was even formed, but merely a determination entered into by less than a dozen gentlemen in the country to protect the person and property of Mr. Hanson, and defend the liberty of the press with their lives if necessary.*

Another rebuttal to the Baltimore City Council investigation that was widely disseminated came from a Federalist newspaper in Boston. The *Boston Repertory* pointed out numerous inconsistencies and noted with sarcasm that the city report on the mob attacks never actually used the word "mob." The rioters were described as "the boys," "the disorderly" or "the assailants." "Better would it have been for the Magistrates of Baltimore to have denied roundly there ever was a MOB...Bold assertions are often more successful than feeble excuses for acknowledged offences," the newspaper wrote.[69]

MADISON AND MONROE WEIGH IN

The Federalists weren't the only ones reacting to news from the investigation. Responses to the flurry of conflicting narratives came even from the highest levels. President James Madison wrote back to the Maryland attorney general in August after the city council report was published, calling it a "seasonable antidote to the misrepresentations" of those who would use the incident for political gain or "factious ambition."[70]

Secretary of State James Monroe struck a somewhat more diplomatic tone in a letter to President Madison the week before. He wrote disapprovingly of the conduct of the Federalists in inciting the mob but stopped short of condoning the mob's actions. "Mobs however must be prevented, & the punishment even of such men as the Editors of that paper must be inflicted by law, not mob movements," he wrote.[71]

Secretary of State James Monroe. *Library of Congress.*

CHARGES FILED AGAINST RIOTERS

The rule of law was also on the minds of Baltimore city leaders. The Monday following the post office attack, the criminal courts reopened. Charges were filed against many of the rioters involved in the Charles Street attack and the jailbreak, including Mumma and Wolleslager. Offenses alleged included unlawful assembly, rioting, forcible entry, vandalism, tarring and feathering and murder. John Bentley, the jail keeper, was charged with neglect of duty in permitting the jail door to be opened. The Federalists did not escape unscathed either. Most of Hanson's band faced multiple charges, including accusations of manslaughter for the deaths of Dr. Thaddeus Gale and John Williams. Hanson and Wagner also stood accused of libel against the government for their original June editorial opposing the war, though the grand jury later found insufficient cause to move forward with that charge.

John Mumma, the butcher, had his day in court later in the month, but it was not quite as he might have expected. Mumma was arrested on unrelated charges for kidnapping and "carrying away" a free black woman. According to news reports, he appeared in court the morning of August 27 to answer those charges, only to have the grand jury return a murder indictment the same day for his role in the death of General Lingan. Mumma was detained and held in custody at the jail, pending a trial scheduled for the following month.[72]

Incarceration of the popular butcher, along with several other alleged co-conspirators, immediately stirred up the mob's ire just as it had finally seemed to be ebbing. Worries of another attempted jailbreak commenced almost immediately. Once he learned of Mumma's indictment, Sheriff Merryman joined Judge Scott, and the pair tracked down the mayor to ask for help. "From what had before taken place, I was apprehensive of danger; and thought it best to summon the posse comitatus immediately," the sheriff recalled.

A large number of citizens gathered at the mayor's house that night to organize in defense of the jail. Major William Barney volunteered for a reconnaissance mission and rode his horse through much of the city to assess the situation, though he was advised not to venture into Fell's Point. General Stricker ordered out the militia, but Mayor Johnson, perhaps hedging his bets based on past experience, also asked the sheriff to prepare his posse to be ready regardless, "as if the military were not to turn out."

The city's Fifth Infantry Regiment did in fact turn out to protect the jail along with an artillery company—fortuitously as it turned out, as the rioters showed up again in force and threatened to break Mumma out of jail. "The first night, it is my opinion, the mob would have taken Mumma out had not the military appeared," Major Barney recalled. The sheriff was also full of praise for the militia's response. "I think [the jail] would have been overturned if the military…had not arrived as soon as it did. I think the artillery companies behaved like soldiers and gentlemen upon that occasion."

MORE THREATS AGAINST NEWSPAPER

While the city remained in turmoil, effects were being felt some thirty-five miles away in Georgetown. Under the direction of Hanson's partner, Jacob Wagner, the *Federal Republican* continued to publish from a building at the corner of Bridge and Washington Streets, just a few miles from the White House, or the President's House, as it was known. Threats against the Georgetown office were reported by a group of workers from Baltimore, who planned to gather in Washington, according to one published report. Citizens in Georgetown rallied to the newspaper's defense, and an armed militia formed to protect the office.[73]

The severity of the actual threat was disputed, and one Republican newspaper accused the Federalists of manufacturing the crisis for political gain. "People of Georgetown—we caution you against receiving too credulously stories calculated to produce a prejudice....Rest assured that no mobs will visit your Town—no threat or preparations of defense are necessary—you will never be attacked," the *National Intelligencer* wrote.

Getting the newspaper to subscribers also continued to be a challenge for the publishers, as the fear of reprisals largely put a stop to any delivery by letter carrier in Baltimore. Wagner felt his rights were being violated and wrote a pair of letters to the U.S. postmaster general to complain.[74] In one letter, Wagner suggested that the *Federal Republican* might soon resume publication in Baltimore rather than rely on the U.S. mail for delivery.

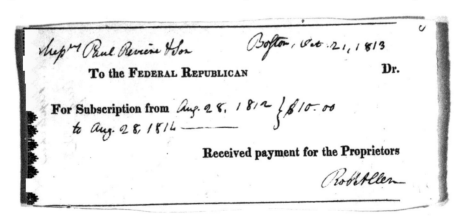

Attempts to silence Hanson's newspaper largely backfired, as Federalists around the county rallied to help by taking out subscriptions. Even seventy-seven-year-old Paul Revere, retired in Boston, paid ten dollars for a two-year subscription. *Massachusetts Historical Society.*

In addition to the human loss and physical toll, Hanson and Wagner also faced mounting financial pressures from the rioting. A prompt return to Baltimore appeared unlikely for financial reasons as much as any other. The destruction of the offices and printing equipment added to their woes, prompting Hanson's friends to pen letters seeking donations for the cause. One such letter addressed to a wealthy Boston resident asked "respectful consideration in the expectation that the federalists in your town may be disposed to contribute."[75]

In a show of solidarity, Federalist supporters outside of Maryland also agreed to take out subscriptions to help keep the paper afloat. The effort worked, and the newspaper's circulation expanded greatly, including more than three hundred new subscribers from Boston and nearly seventy in Providence.[76] Even the seventy-seven-year-old Revolutionary War patriot Paul Revere took out a subscription.[77]

WAR OF WORDS ESCALATES

Another verbal skirmish broke out between the Federalists and Maryland governor Robert Bowie. The governor arrived in Baltimore a few days after the jail massacre and was present at the home of Mayor Johnson on the night of the first post office attack. While much of the political heat generated by the riots focused on the mayor and General Stricker, Bowie, age sixty-two, was quickly drawn into the argument. Many Marylanders living outside of Baltimore already grumbled about the city's outsized role in state affairs, and residents from Federalist-leaning counties in particular expressed little confidence that city leaders were up to the task of properly addressing the rioting. In a series of public meetings held across the state, citizens approved resolutions denouncing the Baltimore mob and calling on Governor Bowie to step in, restore peace and ensure those involved were punished.

At a town meeting in mid-August, Charles County, Maryland residents passed a strongly worded resolution denouncing attempts to "silence the FREEDOM OF THE PRESS by a system of terror and proscription." Prince George's County residents also met and adopted their own resolution with much the same language: "Our indignation has been greatly increased when we have seen that the civil authorities in this state…have been silent spectators of the most atrocious enormities that ever disgraced a civilized community."[78]

One of the earliest gatherings was across the District of Columbia line in Georgetown, where residents gathered on August 7 at the Union Tavern for a meeting chaired by well-known Federalist William Marbury. Their resolution lavished praise on Hanson and General Lingan and invoked the specter of Napoleon: "The attempts to destroy the liberty of the press by the Mob of Baltimore…far exceed in atrocity and violence, the cruel murder by the despot in France"[79]

Federalist fears of the French menace were a recurring theme after the riots and parallels were drawn to Robespierre's Reign of Terror during the French Revolution.

The following week at a Republican meeting chaired by the mayor of Georgetown, a group of residents countered with their own resolutions, claiming that the Federalists' statement did not accurately reflect the views of local citizens. Another Republican meeting was held at a private home in Frederick County, Maryland. Both groups expressed disapproval of the mob but also criticized the divisiveness of the press and issued an appeal to support the government. "Ten thousand pens dipped in gall and wielded by falsehoods and treason are employed to deceive the people and blacken the acts of our public officers," Frederick County Republicans wrote.[80]

A leading Republican newspaper editor even claimed that Federalists had hired men to ride around the countryside in Maryland and neighboring Pennsylvania to spread the "most horrible falsehoods" about the mob attacks. Their goal was to discredit the city and injure its "mercantile and political character," wrote Hezekiah Niles, publisher of the *Niles Weekly Register*, a respected news magazine based in Baltimore.[81]

There's little evidence to support the claim, but some angry Federalists did retaliate with violence of their own. Just days after the jailhouse massacre, a congressman from Duxbury, Massachusetts, was attacked and beaten in neighboring Plymouth by a mob angered by his pro-war vote.[82]

News of the attacks had also spread across the ocean. The *Times of London*, no doubt pleased to be able to embarrass the Madison administration and the anti-British Republican Party, offered nearly a full page of news about the mob attacks, with excerpts of letters from American newspapers. "What are we to think of the laws, or the public feeling, or the liberty of the individual, in a country liable to the outrages we are about to describe?" the paper queried. Another British newspaper in Hereford chided, "The town of Baltimore has been the scene of lawless outrage, rivalling the horrors of the French Revolution."[83]

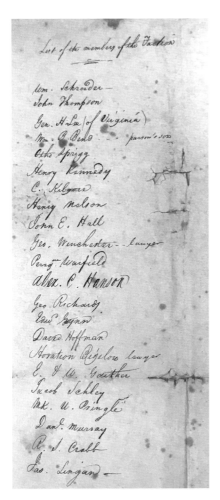

Word of the mob attacks spread outside the city by letter and newspaper. One local resident who shared news with a friend overseas expressed little sympathy for the Federalists, calling them "bravadoes from Montgomery County" and included a list of the "faction" in his letter. *Maryland Historical Society*.

In Hanson's home of Montgomery County, Maryland, a Federalist bulwark, a large gathering including most of the county's delegation to the state assembly as well as residents of "all political parties" met in Rockville. A lengthy public resolution was adopted that mixed in condemnation of Baltimore with approbation for the efforts of the Federalists. "Thanks of this assembly are due to ALEXANDER C. HANSON and his the Heroic Companions who with unexampled bravery and magnanimity risked their lives in defense of this palladium of our Rights."[84] A recommendation was also adopted asking citizens to wear a black band on their left arms for the next thirty days as a tribute General Lingan.

Another gathering was held the same week in the northeastern end of the county at a local tavern, where citizens called for a halt to trade and commerce with Baltimore "until order shall be restored, and the laws of the state again respected in that city." Both resolutions called for a full investigation from the state assembly. Similar pro-Federalist resolutions passed in St. Mary's, Kent, Frederick and Somerset Counties and in the neighboring county of Loudoun, Virginia. Most were published in area newspapers and forwarded to Governor Bowie and other state leaders.

Bowie responded with a lengthy statement of his own in which he declared that order was restored in Baltimore and defended the actions of the mayor and General Stricker. "Those gentlemen not only fulfilled every legal duty incumbent upon them, but made every effort even at the hazard of their lives, to prevent violence," he wrote.[85] The governor called on citizens to unite and show solidarity against the British. Bowie's statement did not satisfy the Federalists, and the sniping continued back and forth in the press.

While the war of words continued, so did the war against Britain. As the month of August drew to a close, residents read the news that the United States' attempted invasion of Canada had ended in disaster. General William Hull miscalculated and was forced to retreat in humiliation, surrendering Fort Detroit with more than two thousand men. Instead of triumphantly marching into Canada as some had predicted, the first major campaign of the war resulted in a loss of territory to the British. Native American tribes, led by Tecumseh, played a key role in manipulating General Hull into believing he was outnumbered.

Hanson himself was focused on other tasks. He had recuperated well enough to travel and was making preparations to pay his last respects to General Lingan. An elaborate funeral was planned in Georgetown, expected to be "a very grand affair." He had written to his wife with instructions to make sure the general's horse and sword were brought so they could be part of the procession, which had to be relocated from a church to an outside venue to accommodate the anticipated crowds.[86] General Lee was still too injured to travel, but most of Hanson's surviving "Spartan Band" planned to attend.

For the Federalists, the funeral would serve as a fitting tribute to their slain friend as well as a convenient rallying cry heading into the fall election season. For Alexander Hanson, it was the perfect opportunity to pivot toward a new challenge: his candidacy for U.S. Congress.

FAREWELLS

*Shall the stranger, my friends, attempt to speak your Hero's praise?—I never fed
at his board, I never drank of his cup....Yet as the brave man who fought the
battles of my country's liberty, is to be the subject of my praise....I would hope
on this day to do honor to his memory.*
—George Washington Parke Custis, on the death of Lingan

GEORGETOWN, SEPTEMBER 1, 1812—Mourners gathered in Georgetown around eleven o'clock to pay their final respects to General James M. Lingan. No church was large enough to accommodate the crowd, so the funeral procession began at the Union Tavern and headed north on Washington Street to Parrott's Woods, about half a mile away. The sounds of church bells and a funeral dirge filled the air, and a "solemn stillness pervaded the streets," one spectator later remembered.[87] Most of the shops were closed, and many storefronts were draped in black. A newly built ship in Georgetown christened the *General Lingan* hung its colors at half-mast and fired off its guns in salute.

Near the front of the procession after the clergy was General Lingan's empty hearse with horses draped in black and pallbearers wearing white scarves. Lingan's son, George, a sixteen-year-old student at Phillips Academy in Andover, Massachusetts,[88] rode behind, followed by the general's own horse—now riderless—and other family members. Major Musgrave, still disfigured from his wounds at the jail massacre, carried the general's sword, and Hanson marched behind him with a number of fellow survivors.

George Washington Parke Custis. *New York Public Library.*

Veterans from the Revolutionary War and other distinguished residents joined the procession, followed by citizens from six different counties and the District of Columbia. Marshals led at the front and rear, and some military troops joined the procession, even though local militia and regular infantry were officially discouraged from turning out. President Madison reportedly felt it improper to have an official military presence, since criminal charges were pending against many of the men marching. Opponents called the move hypocritical, later pointing out that even men killed in duels were honored with military funerals. One unhappy militia officer ordered to disperse by the city's Republican commander responded, "Then take my sword and my commission."[89]

The parade converged at the woods on the outskirts of Georgetown in an open clearing shaded by tall oak trees. A funeral platform was set up for the clergy and speakers, with seats arranged for the audience. The crowd of mourners, numbering as many as two thousand, drew in behind them. Serving as a canopy above the platform was the tent used by George Washington in the Revolution; the tent was "in good preservation, though bearing the marks of six-and-thirty years service."[90]

Lingan's son, daughters and other family filled the front benches—not including his grief-stricken wife, Janet. According to one account, a man wielding a spear-like weapon and a bloody military cap inscribed with the words "Federal Republican" accosted Mrs. Lingan earlier in the morning while she was waiting in her carriage. She broke down in tears and remained at the hotel, unable to attend her husband's service.[91]

Hanson sat near the general's family along with other members of his "Spartan Band." After opening prayers, a eulogy was delivered by George Washington Parke Custis, the adopted son of the late president. Custis was well known for his oratory skills, and he did not disappoint on this day. His three-thousand-word address, delivered mostly extemporaneously, "riveted the attention of the audience; the solemn stillness which reigned was only interrupted by sighs and tears," according to one observer.[92]

In a letter written a short time after the massacre, Hanson reminded his wife, Priscilla, to make arrangements for bringing General Lingan's horse and sword for the funeral ceremony. "There is no doubt the procession will be a very grand affair," he wrote. *Maryland Historical Society*.

After recounting Lingan's heroics during the Revolution, his time on a prison ship and his service after the war, Custis spoke of his role in Hanson's newspaper battle. "He had seen the laws of his country prostrated at the feet of tyrannic power, and the liberty of the press violated, and usurped! And when he saw a band of youth prepare to defend their rights, or perish in the breach, the soul of the veteran rejoiced—'I admire these boys,' he said, 'their heroic ardor reminds me of my other days—I will join their gallant calling.'"[93]

Custis lamented the nation's decline since the "good old federal times" of Washington and noted that the late president would be saddened to witness his fellow soldier's inglorious demise. He portrayed the young Federalists as the "sons of sire" who had picked up the mantle as defenders of freedom from the "grey haired men" who fought for the country's independence. These Federalists were not foreigners or "rakings of kennels" who had just come ashore, he told his audience—a reminder of the class and ethnic divisions that persisted—but rather they "sprang from the oak which had borne the hardest blasts of liberty's storm."

He then described Lingan's final moments after being delivered to the jail, a place designed as an "asylum of justice," which instead became a "chamber of death."

> *Attend the closing scene. The old man falls; yet feebly raising his wounded head, on which three score winters had shed their snows, he appeals to his murderers—"Spare the old man, whose years are few to live! Spare the father, whose orphans will want! Spare the old soldier, whose faithful services, and whose hard sufferings have earned his country's liberties!"*

President Madison was not mentioned by name, but Custis took partisan shots at his administration and cautioned against any effort to cover up the rioting. He pledged that "no veil shall screen this work of darkness from the light of truth" and used part of his speech as a rallying call to fellow Federalists. He warned against the loss of freedom and called it a march to despotism.

The crowd warmly received Custis's eulogy. "Old warriors, who had almost forgotten how to weep, felt the stream of sympathy stealing down their furrowed cheeks,"[94] one spectator later gushed. Copies of his speech were quickly produced, including a pamphlet with footnotes and editorial commentary. Federalists hoped that such eloquent rhetoric might serve as a powerful reminder of the mobs'—and President Madison's—

misdeeds. A Federalist newspaper in Boston even published a poem about Lingan's death:

> *But fairer than light, a meek, sorrowing form.*
> *See Freedom come griev'd and with bosom forlorn*
> *The sad bodings of fear still unite with her moan,*
> *That the death of her Lingan presages her own![95]*

Reaction in the Republican press was muted. A number of newspapers simply republished the text of Custis's remarks without additional commentary. Hanson was easy to attack, but for most Republicans, taking on the scion of President Washington, or Lingan the fallen war hero, was impolitic. One South Carolina newspaper had no such compunction. "A greater compound and farrago of trash and nonsense was never uttered on any solemn occasion before," the paper wrote, encouraging Custis to stick to sheep farming rather than speechmaking.[96]

On Tuesday evening after the funeral ended and many of the mourners had dispersed, Hanson and his fellow Federalists in the funeral party attended a dinner at a local Georgetown tavern. In a long, overflowing banquet room, the men sat down at a series of tables and dined, drank and celebrated. Another group of Federalists from Virginia was seated in an adjoining room and later joined them. After dinner, William Marbury led the men in a series of toasts, and as was often the custom, many were recorded for posterity and later published in the newspaper.

Marbury started with a toast to the memory of General Lingan: "A man worthy of the confidence of Washington." Toasts were offered to the health of General Lee: "May his speedy recover prove to tyrants and usurpers, they yet have honest veterans to combat," and other "Heroes of Charles Street." Hanson rose and offered a toast to the liberty of the press and the right of opinion, "to be maintained, though oceans of 'the best blood of the country' be spilt in the struggle." Another man toasted to a more practical goal: "May the approaching election in Maryland prove an atonement for her past errors and crimes." Dr. Peregrine Warfield, one of the Federalist survivors, toasted Custis, "the orator of the day, he faithfully told the story of our Lingan's virtues and wrongs."[97]

After the toasts, Custis rose from his table and addressed the crowd. He thanked the men for their accolades. "I was bred at Mount Vernon and there learnt to respect integrity, love virtue and venerate the brave," he said. Then he glanced down and spotted a small boy not quite four years old. Custis reached out, clasped the boy in his arms and raised him onto the table. "Here is the scion sprung from the tree which hath borne one of the hardest blasts in Liberty's storms."[98] The young boy's name was Edward Pickering Hanson.

After the tributes ended, Custis invited Hanson to spend time with him at his home. Custis had devoted much of his career to preserving the legacy of his adoptive father, George Washington, and admired the devotion to liberty that Hanson embraced. Custis had built a Greek Revival mansion on the grounds of his 1,100-acre estate across the Potomac River in Arlington. He intended the home, known as the Arlington House, to serve as a tribute to the late president, and it housed many of Washington's artifacts. Work on the property was not yet completed, but Custis was a gracious host and most visitors came away impressed, Hanson among them.

"He gave me a distinguished reception and requested that I would sleep in the very bed on which George Washington drew his last breath," Hanson wrote to his wife, who was still at home in Rockville, now about six months pregnant. Custis also offered Hanson the use of Washington's celebrated tent to use for his Federalist meetings.

The Arlington House as it appeared circa 1864. In a historical twist, the property would later became better known as the home of Robert E. Lee. Custis's daughter married Lee in 1830, and the couple lived in the home until the eve of the Civil War. The Arlington House was used by the Union army during the war; later, the grounds became part of Arlington National Cemetery. *Library of Congress.*

While he was staying in Arlington, Hanson learned of a new development in Baltimore. The grand jury had returned a formal indictment against him and many of his Federalist colleagues for the deaths of Dr. Thaddeus Gale and John Williams. The indictment was not unexpected, and Hanson was relieved to learn he'd be facing charges of manslaughter rather than murder. Manslaughter was a "bailable and not a capital offense," Hanson assured his wife, "you therefore have no reason to be uneasy."

After writing a few more letters, Hanson decided to return home to Rockville the next day. Despite his ongoing health woes, he intended to continue his campaign as the Federalist candidate for Maryland's Third Congressional District, which included Montgomery County and parts of Frederick County. The seat had been held by a Federalist in the prior term and was far more hospitable politically than the city of Baltimore, but the election was contested and Hanson's opponent was a former state assembly member.[99]

Before Lingan's funeral, Hanson had spent time traveling around his district "electioneering and arousing the people," but travel slowed his recovery and his friends grew worried. "It grieves me to learn…that you have been ill, and that there is danger of your recovery being much retarded," wrote fellow Federalist Robert Goodloe Harper. "You must take more care of yourself. Be quiet and tranquil till you are quite well. Your election will take care of itself, or be taken care of by your friends."

Mixed in with his advice were some private words of caution. Harper applauded his friend's staunch principles but was uneasy with his confrontational approach. There are times when the patriot must take risks to protect the free press, he wrote. "But the liberty of the press might, I think, have been defended, and better defended, without coming to Baltimore under the circumstances which existed."[100]

First Mob Trials in Baltimore

Back in Baltimore, the wheels of justice were turning quickly, although not as Hanson would have liked. The month of September began with one of the first trials arising from the mob attacks. William Daley, identified in the city directory as either a grocer or a shoemaker, faced charges for tarring and feathering John Thompson. Daley went on trial September 2, and a jury of twelve men promptly acquitted him. Four other men charged in the attack on Thompson were later found not guilty as well. One juror, Benjamin Bowen, allegedly said that he wouldn't rule against any of the anti-Federalist rioters because "the affray originated with them Tories" and "they all ought to have been killed."

John Mumma, Hugh Beard and Kenelom White were each put on trial for the murder of Lingan. Beard's trial was held first on September 10, and others were spaced out over the span of a week. Attorney General John Montgomery prosecuted the cases. In his opening arguments, Montgomery emphasized the significance of the crime to the jury—"breaking a sanctuary like the jail, and committing murder on an aged man and defenseless prisoner." The evidence presented by witness testimony was strong according to court spectators, and in at least one case, the accused's counsel did not even attempt to mount a formal defense. Montgomery told the jury that if certain facts were proved, the panel must render a verdict of guilty. He then read a passage from the law about the difference between first- and second-degree murder, and the jury retired. The jury pool was nearly identical for each man's trial and so was the verdict: not guilty.

Montgomery told colleagues afterward he was incredulous at the verdicts and felt it was useless to prosecute any more cases in front of the existing jury panel. Critics laid a portion of the blame at Montgomery's feet. Some felt he did not give his full effort. "Whether the Attorney General applied all his ability in the investigation of the cases before him, I cannot say; all that I can feel myself at liberty to say is, that in my opinion, he did not examine the witnesses with that ability which the importance of the occasion demanded," said Nicholas Brice, an attorney who observed the trials.

Others felt it was a moot issue. The jury was predisposed to acquit, and Montgomery's efforts were fruitless. "My impression is, that the jury would not have been influenced by the powers or argument of any one to convict," recalled Thomas Kell, a local attorney. William Gwynn agreed. No impartial trial could be held in the city, he said, "on account of particular prejudices excited by the late disturbances." He urged Montgomery to request the cases be removed to another jurisdiction. Montgomery said there was no precedent for doing so and refused. His position was supported by Judge Scott, who insisted that the power to seek removal belonged to the accused rather than the state.

If Republicans in Baltimore were surprised by the not-guilty verdicts, Federalists outside the city were not. "Thus are murderers let loose upon society in the most turbulent and worst regulated place in America, with all the encouragement to a repetition of their crimes which can arise from a perfect impunity," the *Federal Republican* wrote. A Boston newspaper called the outcome a "mockery of a trial."[101]

The trials continued throughout the month and into October, but the result was the same, even with a new jury pool. Sixteen men were charged with Lingan's murder, including George Wolleslager, and all were acquitted. Dr. Philip Lewis (the French apothecary), Wolleslager and a half dozen other men charged with destroying the *Federal Republican* office during the first attack in June were also acquitted. Two jurors later explained that, despite the evidence, "the persons in Charles Street commenced the riot and deserved punishment."

Only two men were ever convicted of any crime in connection with the mob attacks. Joseph Merriam, an upholsterer, and Frederick Fleming, identified in the city directory as a porter bottler, were both found guilty of rioting and assaulting the Federalist house on Charles Street. Merriam was also convicted of firing a gun into the window of the house. Following jury trials, both men had their cases continued by the court and were then issued fines: ten dollars for Fleming and fifty dollars for Merriam.

Of course, the rioters were not the only ones on trial; Hanson and his fellow Federalists were also facing a variety of charges, including manslaughter. Their attorneys successfully filed motions in mid-September to have the cases removed to Annapolis, a move that Attorney General Montgomery opposed. In contrast to Baltimore, the two political parties were fairly evenly matched in Anne Arundel County, and the attorney general and many others feared the Federalists would escape justice. "In conversation he told me he thought they were guilty of willful and deliberate murder. Where he wished the trials to take place, I did not hear him say," Nicholas Brice recalled.

The change in venue gave the Federalists a better shot at legal vindication, but acquittal was by no means certain. For Hanson, there was another obstacle to be dealt with. His political opponents were trying to use his manslaughter indictment to argue he was ineligible to run for Congress. Before Hanson could clear his name in the criminal court, he had to deal with the court of public opinion.

DECISION DAY

It is a fact, that the Federalists at Baltimore assembled first, armed in defiance of the people and contrary to the laws.
It is fact, that the Federalists fired first upon the people of Baltimore.
It is a fact, that the Federalists killed two and the people of Baltimore one.
It is a fact, that the coroner's inquest declared the killing of the two people by the Federalists premeditated murder.
—Easton Republican Star, *September 1, 1812*

ROCKVILLE, SEPTEMBER 20, 1812—Alexander Hanson knew the next month held the key to his fate; a trial for manslaughter and his congressional election would both be decided within the span of a fortnight in early October. The pressure was weighing on him. Writing from his home in Rockville, Hanson attempted to share his feelings in a letter to a Baltimore bookseller. His mind was "troubled"—why would "merciful providence" spare his life during the mob massacre, only for him to "witness the humiliation of federalism," he questioned.[102]

The Republican press had battered Hanson and his fellow Federalists starting almost immediately after the jail massacre. They repeatedly accused him of manipulating the riots for political gain. "Nothing can be more ridiculous than the awkward attempts made to enlist the late outrages in Baltimore into the services of the opponents of the government," the *National Intelligencer* wrote.

Roger Brooke Taney later abandoned the Federalist Party, and a lengthy career in state and national politics followed, capped off by an appointment as chief justice of the U.S. Supreme Court. Today, his court tenure is most remembered for what is widely considered the worst decision in the court's history. In *Dred Scott v. Sanford*, Taney wrote the majority opinion declaring that slaves could not be U.S. citizens or have standing in federal courts. The decision was a controversial one, even at the time. Upon Taney's death, when the question arose whether Congress should pay to commission a marble bust as was tradition, U.S. Senator Charles Sumner famously remarked that Taney should be "hooted down the pages of history." *Library of Congress.*

Much was made of a letter written to Hanson prior to his return to Baltimore in July. Augustus Taney, a Federalist from Fredrick County, advised Hanson not to follow through on his plans to revive the newspaper in the city. The law will not allow you to take the "sword of justice" into your own hands, Taney warned. "To fire on the assailants before other means of putting them out of the house have been used, would be unlawful and subject us to the punishment of manslaughter," he wrote, citing advice from his brother, Roger Brooke Taney, an attorney and candidate for Congress in the neighboring district.[103]

Once the letter was made public, Hanson's opponents pounced. In their eyes, it was proof that the Federalists knew full well what they were in for and purposefully provoked the mob. The real rioters were the "armed banditti" in the Charles Street house, the *Baltimore Sun* argued. "Intents and act prove the conspirators guilty of murder," wrote the *Baltimore Whig*. The *Republican Star* of Easton said the letters were proof of Federalist premeditation, which the "Tory press" was attempting to cover up. "We propose laying the truth before the proper judges, the PEOPLE; they by its suppression and the substitution of falsehood," wrote the *Star*.

Hanson tried to downplay the Taney letter, claiming it was "disingenuously perverted to an unjust and infamous purpose," but it was clear a more forceful response was necessary. He assembled a team of prominent attorneys to help make his case. They included Walter Dorsey, Robert Goodloe Harper, Thomas Buchanan and Phillip Barton Key. Dorsey, who had led the effort to bail the Federalists from jail before the massacre, was a former chief justice of the Baltimore courts. Key was the incumbent member of Congress whose seat Hanson was seeking to fill. Harper was a well-known Federalist leader, and Buchanan was a respected Baltimore attorney.

The attorneys penned a legal opinion that was published in the *Federal Republican* and other newspapers and prefaced by a lengthy message from Hanson to the voters of his congressional district. "My late attempt to restore the right of opinion and revive the Liberty of the Press in Maryland has been grossly misrepresented," Hanson wrote. He apologized for not being able to get out meet voters in person, which he attributed to the effects of the "brutal violence" suffered in Baltimore. "I am, therefore compelled to adopt this mode of addressing you, with a view of counter-acting…these insidious efforts," he wrote.[104]

Hanson recounted the details of the mob attack on the Charles Street house and stressed that he and his band had only used force when they had no other option to defend themselves. "Would you rather kill or be murdered?" he asked readers.

After sharing his views on the subject, he concluded with a direct appeal to the voters:

> *If you wish to give them your countenance and support, I shall be proud to become your representative. But if you are prepared, which I cannot and will not believe, to calculate the cost of when your liberties are to be defended, if you mean to submit to the first and the successive encroachments of tyranny for fear of the inconvenience or hazard of resistance, I am free to declare I am not a fit object for your choice.*

Hanson's lengthy campaign statement was followed by an opinion from his attorneys, whom he called "some of the most eminent counselors of law in the country." They addressed several legal issues raised, including whether Hanson's pending indictment for manslaughter could prevent him from running for or serving in Congress. In their view, no such legal disqualification existed. "To admit a mere accusation, which may on trial appear to be false, as a disqualification for a citizen to be elected as a member of Congress, would be equally contrary to every principle of justice, law and common sense," they wrote.

The timing of events was such that Hanson's congressional election would take place during the first week of October, with his trial expected the following week in Annapolis, in neighboring Anne Arundel County.

ELECTION DAY ARRIVES

When Election Day arrived on Monday, October 5, Hanson likely ventured over to the county courthouse in Rockville to vote. The Third District was one of nine congressional seats in Maryland; it included all of Montgomery County and parts of Frederick County east of Frederick town, dancing up to the Pennsylvania line.

In Montgomery County, there were five voting districts, though two of them may have shared the same location. Polls opened from nine o'clock in the morning until six o'clock in the evening. The folded ballots, either handwritten or printed, were stuffed into the ballot box, and a local judge or clerk recorded the names of voters in a poll book. Once the polls closed, the box was opened in public view and the votes were tallied. Under state election law, ballots that were "deceitfully" folded together or ballots with more than the proscribed number of candidates were not to be counted.[105]

Results were often announced the same evening, though it might take longer before news reached other voting areas. By Wednesday, the *Federal Republican* had the full results for Montgomery County. Hanson's opponent edged him out in the Rockville voting district, 216–150, but he more than made up the margin in the rest of the county. Two days later, the full results were published, showing Hanson carrying Frederick County and winning the seat by more than 900 votes. Different outlets reported minor discrepancies in the totals, but the final returns gave Hanson a comfortable winning margin.

Third Congressional District	A. Hanson	J. Linthicum
Rockville Courthouse	153	216
Berry's	204	87
Goshen	398	167
Medley's	255	84
Montgomery County	**1,010**	**554**
Buckey's Town	81	22
Liberty Town	567	255
New Market	302	184
Taneytown	386	203
Westminster	245	488
Frederick County	**1,581**	**1,152**
Total	**2,591**	**1,706**

Results for Maryland's Third Congressional District in 1812. Linthicum appears to have run without a formal party designation, but in this case, he became the de facto Republican candidate. *A New Nation Votes, Tufts University Digital Collections Archive and American Antiquarian Society.*

The balance of the Maryland's congressional delegation remained unchanged at 6-3 in favor of the Republicans—a fact Federalists blamed on the practice of gerrymandering, a new term first coined earlier that year in Massachusetts. "So adroitly have the districts been carved in the true Gerrymander fashion, that the number of [Republican] members is in an inverse ratio to the relative number of [Republicans] in the state," the *Federal Republican* complained.

The more immediate impact could be seen in the state assembly. Riding a crest of antiwar sentiment driven home by the jail massacre, Hanson and his Federalist Party rebounded from years of exile to retake the reins of power in Maryland. Republican fears that the Baltimore mob attacks might be used as a political wedge turned out to be well founded. Heading into the election, Republicans held a majority in the House of Delegates by a twelve-vote margin, but the Federalist wave that Hanson helped foment swept them out of power. Two of Hanson's cohorts from the jail massacre, Richard J. Crabb and Charles Kilgore, were elected to the assembly, and four previously Republican counties flipped, giving Federalists a 56–24 advantage. The fifteen-member Senate was selected a year earlier and remained in Republican hands, but the Federalist margin in the House was wide enough that for the first time in a dozen years they could control the agenda.

News of the election quickly traveled up the coast and across the ocean to London. The Federalist triumph was hailed as a victory for peace by supporters. "There is much consolation in the rays of political light which have burst from the recent elections," the *Maryland Gazette* wrote. "The State Completely Regenerated" capped a letter published in the *Federal Republican*. A Federalist newspaper in Boston called the election "highly auspicious to the cause of freedom." Of course, the Republicans had a different view. "It appears that…A. C. Hanson of Lathing-Hatchet memory has been elected to represent the TORY county of Montgomery in Maryland," a South Carolina newspaper sarcastically commented.

In Maryland, the implications of the election were enormous. With control of the assembly came the power to select the state's next governor, U.S. senators and the influential governor's council. It also guaranteed a more rigorous investigation of the Baltimore riots.

The Federalist wave was not confined to Maryland. Opposition to the war galvanized support, and the party realized gains in Congress, mostly in New England and the mid-Atlantic states. But since there was no uniform congressional election date—some states held their election in December or even the early part of the next year—it was still too early to know the full impact. Complicating matters was the fact that the House of Representatives was expanding by forty seats following the most recent national census.

Keeping a watchful eye over it all was President James Madison. His own fate would soon be decided once members of the Electoral College were selected and the Maryland results did not augur well. In a letter to Thomas Jefferson written a week after the election, Madison ruminated over his prospects in the various states and noted the outcome in Maryland. "In this State the issue is not favorable," he wrote.[106]

Alexander Hanson did not have much time to bask in his victory, and he soon packed his bags for Annapolis. He'd earned a seat in Congress—now his trial for manslaughter would decide whether he'd be allowed to sit in it.

HANSON ON TRIAL

The triumph of liberty is now complete.

ANNAPOLIS, OCTOBER 7, 1812—Overlooking the harbor in Annapolis with a view of the Chesapeake Bay, the Anne Arundel County Courthouse was a plain rectangular building that doubled as an armory. The Maryland State House stood adjacent, a much more elaborate and attractive brick building featuring a recently repaired dome—apparently more pleasing than the prior iteration, which one architectural critic said "must hurt the eye of every spectator."[107] Nearby, a smaller octagonal building known as the "temple" served as a public bathroom.

For Alexander Hanson, still facing manslaughter charges and a potential ten-plus-year sentence, the return to Annapolis came as a welcome relief. It was not that Annapolis was such fertile Federalist territory. In fact, the city had just elected a full slate of Republicans to the assembly and reelected a Republican member of Congress, much like Baltimore. But most of the similarities ended there.

Annapolis was the state's seat of government, Baltimore the center of commerce. Annapolis was a small, pastoral city with aristocratic roots steeped in historical tradition; Baltimore was a bustling seaport fueled by explosive growth and an influx of immigrants. Annapolis, with about two thousand residents, including slaves and free African Americans, was just a fraction of the size of its sister city. Baltimore, with a deeper channel, was better situated as a seaport, and as a result, the maritime trade that fueled its growth over the past quarter century had largely bypassed Annapolis.

The Maryland State House in Annapolis. Not merely content to challenge Annapolis for economic supremacy, Baltimore had also attempted to claim the mantle of state capital on several occasions. In 1782, a measure to move the seat of government to Baltimore was defeated by a margin of one vote in the state assembly; other attempts would follow. One of the most forceful voices in opposition to the effort was Hanson's father. *New York Public Library.*

Hanson's affinity for Annapolis was strengthened by his shared resentment of Baltimore's outsized influence in state affairs, a bond just as strong as any political affiliation. His late father's home was located nearby, and Hanson had also spent time studying at St. John's College, a short distance from the statehouse.

Hanson was due in court on Wednesday, October 7, along with the twenty co-defendants who had their cases transferred from Baltimore. Presiding over the case would be Jeremiah Townley Chase, chief judge of the Third Judicial District, which included Anne Arundel County. Sitting with him were two associates judges, Richard Hall Harwood and Richard Ridgely. In his mid-sixties with locks "white as snow," Judge Chase was a senior figure in the Maryland legal community and had previously served as a delegate in the Continental Congress, a prosecutor, a senate elector and mayor of Annapolis.[108] He was known to have held anti-Federalist views in his career and was close to Governor Bowie, a Republican, but by most accounts was a respected jurist—"kind, temperate and a sincere Christian," according to one account.[109]

The first two days of court were consumed by motions and procedural matters. One of the first orders of business was to formally admit the lawyers

Left: Judge Jeremiah Townley Chase. *New York Public Library.*

Right: Walter Dorsey. *Library of Congress.*

for each side. Walter Dorsey led the Federalist defense. Prosecuting the case was James Boyle, a former state assemblyman for Annapolis. Boyle carried with him a letter signed by Maryland attorney general John Montgomery attesting to his "integrity, abilities and legal knowledge." Both attorneys were then sworn in after affirming their oaths and declaring their "belief in the Christian religion."[110]

A MOVE TO REMOVE

The first issue for the court to decide was on the removal order itself. The prosecution argued that the transfer of the cases from Baltimore to Annapolis was improper on technical grounds. Boyle asked the judge to reverse the order because the request had come from the defendants' attorney rather than the individuals accused. The judge sided with the Federalists, and the court soon moved on to a thornier matter—juror selection.

The standard process for juror selection in criminal trials was described in an 1809 state law. A list of twenty potential jurors was drawn up and given to both the prosecution and the defense. Each side was allowed to strike four names from the list (known as a peremptory challenge), and the twelve remaining jurors were empaneled for the trial. Challenges for cause were also allowed, and if the pool of jurors dropped below twenty, bystanders might be called to serve by the local sheriff. A separate section of the law applied to capital cases and cases where the accused faced a sentence "for five years at the least." In such instances, the defendant was afforded up to twenty peremptory challenges.

This distinction was a point of contention between the prosecution and the defense. The charge of manslaughter carried a sentence of "not more than ten years." Did such a sentence qualify as "five years at the least?" Specifics of the prosecution's argument are unknown, but it is likely Boyle argued the defendants should only get the standard four challenges rather than twenty. It was no trivial matter. The outcome of the trial might hang in the balance.

The issue occupied the court's time longer than the removal question. After hearing arguments from both sides, the judges retired for the day to consider the matter. The next day, the court decided in favor of the Federalists, clearing the decks for the first trial to get underway on Friday.

The first case to be heard was that of Daniel Murray, Hanson's brother-in-law. The state lined up seventeen witnesses to testify against him, including an interpreter for one of the witnesses. The prosecution witnesses included Thomas Jenkins, the next-door neighbor on Charles Street; Peter White, son of the landlady who rented the house to the Federalists; Andrew Boyd, the sympathetic banker who tried to intervene; John L. Potts, a local flour merchant who observed the mob attack; and Judge John Smith.

The defense also called a handful of witnesses, including Henry Gaither, the Federalist who escaped in the confusion during the march to the jail; Dr. John Owen, who treated the wounded at the jail; and John Abell, a local magistrate who tried to stop the mob.

HENRY GAITHER TAKES THE STAND

Much of the witness testimony has not survived, so the substance is unknown. Some accounts were taken in shorthand and later republished in local newspapers, including that of Peter White, John Worthington and Henry Gaither. The *Federal Republican* devoted a full page to Gaither's testimony due to "its precise detail and the well-known respectability of the witness." Despite any built-in bias, the detailed summary offers a window into the trial.

Judge Harwood administered the oath to Gaither. "You are sworn to relate the truth, and the whole truth relative to the case now before the jury," he said. Gaither then launched into a lengthy narrative describing his involvement at the Charles Street house. When he reached the point where the mob began to gather outside the house, he was interrupted by the prosecutor. Boyle questioned whether the group assembled in front of the house wasn't actually just boys?

"There might have been some boys, though I thought the most of them men," Gaither replied.

Boyle followed up by asking how many men were inside the house, alluding to what had become a common Republican attack line since the riots: the Federalists were armed and prepared for battle, hardly the innocent bystanders they claimed to be.

"I cannot say how many were in the house—they were posted in different rooms at the time I first entered the house," Gaither answered, but did not offer a number.

Gaither continued his testimony, with occasional questions from the defense attorneys as well as the judge and concluded at the point when the city leaders negotiated their transfer to the jail.

The witnesses' testimony consumed most of the day, and the court adjourned to Saturday morning to conclude the case. Murray's attorneys must have felt optimistic about his chances because they did not offer a closing argument and opted to submit the case directly to the twelve-member jury, according to one report.

The verdict was returned without the jury even leaving the box—not guilty. The crowd of spectators erupted in applause. "Such was the joy expressed on his acquittal," one spectator recalled, "the Court-House rang with shouts of joy and huzzas."

After Murray's acquittal, the remainder of the twenty cases were consolidated, and Judge Chase gaveled the court back into session on Monday morning at ten o'clock. Ten of the jurors were held over from Murray's trial with two new members added. The prosecution cut down its witness list, but the defense added a number of new witnesses, including such notable citizens as Samuel Sterett, John Worthington, Christopher Raborg, Richard Dorsey and Nicolas Brice. In all, there were eighteen defense witnesses, more than double the number called for Daniel Murray's defense.

After the resounding verdict in the first criminal case, the Federalists could not have been overly concerned about their fate. Yet the trial still dragged

The original Baltimore court docket showing the charges against the Federalists. All but one of Hanson's fellow Federalists were charged with two counts of manslaughter, one each for the deaths of Thaddeus Gale and John Williams. One of the men, John M. Zollickoffer, was charged only for the death of Williams. *Maryland State Archives.*

on for two more days to accommodate all the witness testimony. It seemed Hanson was not content merely to win the case but saw the opportunity to answer his critics on the public stage. Worthington's testimony in particular cast many of Hanson's foes in a negative light.

When asked about his testimony, Worthington later expressed admiration for Hanson and the Federalists for standing on their principle. "I often regretted that I was not one of those gentlemen—that I thought any person, who wished his name to descend to posterity with glory, ought to envy those gentlemen," he said.

The trial wrapped up on Wednesday afternoon, and once again, the jury did not need to leave its box to render a verdict. Hanson and his cohorts were all acquitted. As before, the spectators applauded. "Thus has ended the fiend like persecution, which those who miraculously escaped murder and assassination have been followed," the *Federal Republican* pronounced. "The triumph of liberty is now complete."

Acquittals were entered on the court docket for all twenty-one defendants. The clerk must have tired of hand-writing the details for each case because at one point he confused Alexander Hanson with Alexander Magruder, a Federalist member of the Governor's Council.

FEDERALIST REDEMPTION

The next afternoon, a public dinner and ball were hosted by the local chapter of the Washington Society, a civic organization that promoted the legacy of George Washington and politicked for Federalist causes. An estimated 120 people gathered at three o'clock in the assembly hall in Annapolis to honor Hanson and celebrate the Federalists' acquittal. The mood in the room was jovial. "Every countenance was illuminated with smiles of unfeigned joy evincing the deep interest which had been excited by the trial, and gratification which all felt at its glorious issue," the *Federal Republican* later explained.

After the dinner, a series of prepared toasts were offered. They included words of praise for the jury and toasts to the memory of George Washington, Alexander Hamilton and James Lingan. Glasses were raised to the Liberty of the Press ("the honor and body guard of civil and political liberty") the Freedom of Discussion ("restrained by the constitutional laws, not by Riotous Mobs") and a sarcastic salute to President Madison, ("may his retreat to Montpelier be speedy, that his country may be released from French Bondage").

The tenth toast was to Alexander Hanson and his cohorts: "a Spartan Band who have sealed with their blood the principles our ancestors transmitted to us." After the toast, Hanson rose and spoke to the crowd in a "most affecting address." When he was done, he raised his glass and offered a toast of his own to the city of Annapolis, comparing the need to clean up the city to Hercules's task in Greek mythology. "When the Augean Stable is cleansed it will be what is was, the seat of science, elegance and refinement of manners," he said. The audience heartily applauded, and more speeches and toasts followed.

If redemption was the theme of Hanson's toast, it might just as well apply to his own fortunes. The night of celebration capped off a remarkable turn of events for the young editor. Only ten weeks earlier, his life hung in the balance as he was unceremoniously dumped into a heap of bodies on the steps of the Baltimore Jail. Now he was headed off to Washington as a newly elected member of Congress who would have a powerful new platform to speak out against the war. His fight to defend the freedom of the press was vindicated, and his Federalist Party was seemingly reborn.

For twenty-six-year-old Alexander Contee Hanson, the future looked bright.

EPILOGUE

ALEXANDER HANSON

The career of Alexander Hanson did burn brightly, but its glow was brief. Hanson's combative, uncompromising style was ill-suited to the politics of Washington, and he quickly angered his colleagues in the Democratic-Republican Congress by demanding extra floor space for newspaper reporters in the Capitol. Hanson remained a thorn in the side of Speaker Henry Clay (and his successor) throughout his tenure and, during one tense moment, even got in a physical altercation with a pro-war member of Congress from North Carolina.

Hanson. *Library of Congress*.

Hanson's recurring ailments from the jail massacre also limited his effectiveness. Following one eagerly anticipated speech against a war financing bill, Hanson collapsed in his seat and began spitting up blood, which forced him to miss the rest of the debate. The opposition party in Baltimore used him as a poster child for the Federalist menace, motivating the electorate by warning what a reelected Hanson might do with "a horde of legislative janizaries at his heels."[111]

At one time, Hanson was heralded along with young Daniel Webster as the vanguard of a new generation of Federalist leaders; he even drew favorable comparisons with the late Alexander Hamilton. Each possessed "the same undisguised frankness, the same warmth of heart; the same lofty daring; the same contempt of danger....[F]ew have excited warmer friendships, or more rancorous enmities," one New York newspaper proclaimed.[112] Webster himself had high praise for his Federalist colleague. "Hanson is a hero," he wrote to a friend in New York in 1813.[113]

As evidence of his growing fame, Hanson's likeness was even included in a traveling "wax work" exhibition featuring life-size figures of Napoleon, George Washington and Christopher Columbus as well as a replica scene of the mob attack at the Baltimore Jail with a wax version of Hanson and his "Spartan Band."[114]

Hanson was reelected and later promoted to U.S senator, one of the youngest in history, but his career never took off. He grew disillusioned with Washington and even his own party and may have suffered from depression. (He grieved the loss of his sister and four children, including a son, James, named after General Lingan, "who winged his way to the mansions of bliss" at a young age.)[115]

Hanson's name was frequently invoked in British newspapers, and his speeches may have helped push Great Britain toward peace, despite holding what some perceived as the stronger hand.[116] Hanson's fierce antiwar views had propelled his career, but its unsatisfying conclusion also appeared to sap his vigor. In one of his final acts as a senator, in 1819, he voted to ratify a treaty with Great Britain to restore relations between the two nations. It was fitting closure for a man who made his career opposing the war.

Two months later, at his country estate in Elkridge, Maryland, known as Belmont, Hanson died quietly at the age of thirty-three. His funeral was attended by a "respectable number of gentlemen," and his passing was duly noted in the press, but with little fanfare compared to the deaths of Lingan and Lee. History has treated him much the same.

Priscilla Hanson was widowed at a young age but still surrounded by her family. Her elder sister Mary lived nearby with her husband, Daniel Murray, at their estate known as Rockburn. Her brother-in-law Charles W. Hanson, a judge, also lived nearby in Baltimore, but he later developed an opium addiction and by 1830 was determined to be in a "deranged state of mind."[117]

Priscilla inherited her husband's estate, with assets valued at $4,406, much of which originally came from her own family. Hanson was a gifted

Hanson's son Charles Grosvenor Hanson was his only child to live to adulthood and have heirs. He is buried with his family in a small cemetery located in the back of the Belmont estate in Elkridge, Maryland, along with other Hanson and Dorsey family members. Hanson himself is also believed to be buried on-site, but the precise location is unknown. Ground-penetrating radar was used in 2014 in an attempt to locate additional burial sites, but the findings were inconclusive. *Photo by the author.*

wordsmith, but his money-management skills were scant and most of his holdings had come from his father or father-in-law. He owed a $3,000 note at the time of his death, and two friends who co-signed the loan later brought a creditor claim against his estate.[118]

An inventory of Hanson's estate included about a dozen slaves ranging in age from "Old Prince," aged eighty, to six-year-old Mary, who was to be freed when she reached the age of thirty-one. Some of the slaves, including Esther, age fifty-five, and Hagar, age thirty-five, fit the description of slaves owned by Priscilla's father. Other assets included sixteen portraits and pictures valued at $100, a bathing tub listed at $75, an old piano at $5, five feather beds for $150, a $20 timepiece and four hay rakes valued at $0.25 each. Some of the highest-priced assets inventoried were the farm goods, including wheat, rye and pork collectively valued at $610.[119]

Priscilla was able to live off the proceeds from the farm at Belmont and the note from the sale of the *Federal Republican* for a time, but eventually, she ran into financial difficulties. She twice sold off portions of her land and, in 1839, mortgaged the estate for $1,500.[120] There is no record that Priscilla ever remarried, and she died at the age of sixty in 1849.

Few of Hanson's children survived to adulthood. His oldest living son, **Edward Pickering Hanson**, died in July 1829 at his mother's home in Anne Arundel County at the age of twenty. Hanson's son **Charles Grosvenor Hanson** was the only child to live a full life and have heirs.

An examination of the life of Alexander Hanson must acknowledge that the man who so defiantly defended liberty and freedom of the press was also a slaveholder. Many years after his death, a former Massachusetts Federalist would defend Hanson as one of a select number of southern legislators who were sympathetic to the Free States and "destitute of a desire to establish the supremacy of slaveholders."[121] Nonetheless, Hanson owned or inherited a dozen or more slaves and relied to some extent on slave labor for his farm and business. One of his slaves was later freed, but there is no evidence that he made any attempts to free the others; in fact, there were a dozen included in his estate at his death. Hanson was not shy about using his newspaper and his platform in Congress to advance political causes, but there is no record he ever did so to speak out against slavery. His newspaper did later help promote the Maryland chapter of the American Colonization Society, which sought to resettle free black residents to West Africa. The effort was intended by some to offer a remedy for slavery, but its motivations were decidedly mixed.[122]

GENERAL "LIGHT-HORSE HARRY" LEE

General "Light-Horse Harry" Lee never recovered from the injuries he sustained during the Baltimore Jail massacre. In the spring of 1813, he left his family and sailed for the West Indies in the hopes that the warmer climate would relieve his suffering. A temporary visit grew permanent, and he spent the next four years in the Caribbean. He kept in touch with his family and corresponded about the war and other political matters, often expressing his frustrations with the course of the war and his own station. "Bitter as are my reflections…I forget my own sorrows in those of our afflicted Country," he wrote from Barbados in the fall of 1813.[123] He sent letters to President Madison and even tried to broker peace with Great Britain directly, but most of his correspondence went unanswered.

Lee traveled around the islands and his health occasionally improved, but he did not feel strong enough to return home. He did keep in touch with his children and frequently expressed regret that he was not there to watch them grow up. While he was not physically present, he tried to offer guidance and advice from afar. "Read, therefore, the best poets, the best orators and the best historians; as from them you draw principles of moral truth, axioms of prudence, and material for conversation," he wrote to one of his older sons from Caicos in the fall of 1816. He encouraged his children to write back more often and inquired of others how they were developing. Lee was particularly concerned about his two young sons, Smith and Robert, and asked about their "disposition to learn, their diligence, and perseverance." In February 1817, he wrote again, asking about young Robert. "And how is my last in looks and understanding? Robert was always good, and will be confirmed in his happy turn of mind by his ever-watchful and affectionate mother. Does he strengthen his native tendency?"[124]

Lee. *Smithsonian Institution*.

By the fall of 1817, with his health in rapid decline, Lee decided the tropical climate could do him no more good, and he determined to return home to his family. After some delays, he boarded a schooner leaving Nassau early the next year and headed for Virginia. The ship stopped at Cumberland Island off the coast of Georgia, and a frail Lee was rowed to shore at Dungeness landing. "He was pale, emaciated, very weak and evidently suffering much pain," according to one observer. Lee convalesced at the home of a friend on the island but never recovered and was unable to complete his journey home.[125]

Lee had famously eulogized President Washington with the words "First in war, first in peace, and first in the hearts of his countrymen" but his own ending was less memorable. Confined to bed with recurring pain, a "depressed and irritable" Lee succumbed to his injuries from the "Mobtown" massacre on March, 25, 1818. He never did get to see his family again, and his son **Robert E. Lee** grew up without knowing his father.

MAYOR EDWARD JOHNSON AND GENERAL JOHN STRICKER

Johnson. *Maryland Historical Society.*

Photo by the author.

The careers of Mayor Edward Johnson and General John Stricker both continued after their clash with Alexander Hanson and the mob. Mayor Johnson was reelected in 1814 and helped guide the city's defenses during the tumultuous war period, including the British bombardment of Fort McHenry that inspired Francis Scott Key's "Star-Spangled Banner." Johnson, a doctor and brewer by trade, also helped establish an asylum for the poor and oversaw major infrastructure improvements in the city.

Following a brief retirement after the war, Johnson returned to the mayor's office twice more and served in a variety of other roles. His efforts to combat a yellow fever epidemic in 1819 were widely applauded, which included publication of a voluminous medical treatise documenting the epidemic. Johnson eventually retired from political life and died in 1829 at age sixty-two. The *Niles Register* noted his death with high praise, calling him "one of the most benevolent men who ever lived." Later, a bronze plaque highlighting Johnson's career was placed outside the site of his former Baltimore home; it notes that the mayor was "nearly killed trying to quell a mob that tried to break into the City Jail and lynch pro-British citizens."

Stricker. *Maryland Historical Society*.

General John Stricker also found redemption in the war. He was harshly criticized for his actions (or lack thereof) during the mob attacks; a Maryland state assembly investigation report said he "failed to do his duty to his country" and was "guilty of a manifest departure from every principle of prudence." Defenders, including the general's son, later claimed that bitter partisanship was to blame for making Stricker "an object of particular resentment," but it was his heroic actions in war that washed away any lingering stain.

In the fall of 1814, shortly after the sacking of Washington, the British infantry marched on Baltimore with similar intent. Stricker, as brigadier general, led the Maryland militia's Third Brigade to defend North Point, a strategically important peninsula outside the city. He succeeded in delaying British advances and claiming the life of a key British army commander in the process. The Battle at North Point bought precious time for the American forces to bolster their defenses at Fort McHenry and defend the city—which ultimately proved a turning point in the war. Stricker was widely praised for his leadership.

Mayor Johnson's city council passed a resolution honoring Stricker's actions and commissioned a portrait to be hung in the council chamber. The Federalists had not forgotten Stricker's perfidy, however, and he was bypassed for a promotion in favor of Hanson ally Robert Goodloe Harper. Stricker resigned his post in protest and returned to his banking career. He remained active in civic life after the war, though later turned down an opportunity to serve in the state senate. The general's health deteriorated, and he died on June 23, 1825, reportedly dropping dead abruptly while his daughter prepared dinner.[126]

JOHN "THE BUTCHER" MUMMA

John "the Butcher" Mumma later expressed remorse for his role in the jailhouse massacre during an unplanned encounter with Hanson's onetime colleague in Congress **Representative Daniel Webster**. During a journey

Daniel Webster. *Library of Congress.*

to Washington in May 1813, Webster was delayed by a broken-down carriage and had to stop outside Baltimore. He found himself in a village at a local tavern and inquired if there was a driver for hire who might take him to the city. Arrangements were made, and when Webster got aboard the carriage, he found none other than John Mumma perched in the driver's seat. After riding a short distance in silence, the Federalist leader and the Mobtown henchman engaged in a conversation that was later retold and published.[127]

Mumma recognized Webster and asked him if he knew who he was. "You are John Mumma, the butcher, the man who killed General Lingan," the congressman reportedly replied.

"Are you not afraid to ride with me, at this time of night?" Mumma asked.

Webster shook his head, and Mumma then explained that he volunteered to drive the carriage so that he could share his story and "free my mind about those Baltimore riots." He had been misled and caught up in the frenzy, he explained, and committed an act he now regretted. By the time Mumma finished, the men had arrived in Baltimore. Webster was dropped off by the door of his hotel, but when he offered to pay for the ride Mumma declined, saying he was glad to finally have the chance to tell his story.

Another Mumma footnote occurred in 1820, a year after Hanson's death. The Republican Party had reassumed power in Maryland, and Mumma was appointed as a justice of the peace in Baltimore. The irony that the former "Butcher of Mobtown" was now a peace officer was not lost on the Federalists. "Is this madness? Or is it revenge?" asked the *Easton Gazette*, calling the move "one of the most aggravating acts of wickedness that has yet been done."

While relatively little is known about the life of John Mumma, the career of Daniel Webster is richly chronicled. At one time, both he and Alexander Hanson were viewed as the rising stars of the Federalist Party, but only Webster's career fulfilled its promise. The onetime New Hampshire representative eventually moved to Massachusetts, where he also served in Congress, and later as a U.S. senator and as secretary of state under three different presidents. A noted legal scholar, Webster also argued cases before the U.S. Supreme Court, including the famous contracts clause case *Dartmouth College v. Woodward*.

While few would question Hanson's courage putting his life on the line to defend the free press, it is Webster's political courage that is celebrated today. In 1850, Webster helped pass a slavery compromise bill that he knew would end his Senate career, but it helped keep the Union together—for a time. His efforts were recognized a century later by John F. Kennedy, who chronicled Webster's valiance in a chapter of his Pulitzer Prize–winning book *Profiles in Courage*.

GENERAL JAMES M. LINGAN

In the months and years after his death, the name of General James Lingan was frequently invoked for political purposes, as a Federalist cudgel against the opposing Republican Party. As time passed and the influence of the Federalist Party waned, he was remembered more as a historical figure—the war hero who died defending the free press against the Baltimore mob. Retrospective coverage of the attacks invariably cited Lingan's name first, before that of General Lee or Hanson himself, likely due to his status as a war hero and the fact that he was the only one of the "Spartan Band" who perished during the actual attack; it took much longer for Lee and Hanson to succumb to their injuries.

Lingan. *Maryland Historical Society*.

In November 1908, at the request of Lingan's granddaughters, his body was disinterred from the burying ground in Georgetown and moved to Arlington National Cemetery. The granddaughters feared that his private grave might be lost to history and felt Arlington was a more fitting site. Lingan's bones were placed along with those of his wife in a grave at one of the "most beautiful spots in Arlington." A newspaper account at the time reported the move in macabre detail, noting that "the fracture in the skull of the long dead hero is still visible."[128]

Lingan's name was included in a national monument to slain journalists erected in Arlington, Virginia, in 1996. Glass panels were etched with the names of each journalist and arranged in a spiral overlooking the Potomac River. Originally, 934 journalists from around the world were included, and Lingan's death in 1812 was the first documented case. "We want to call attention to the risks journalists face in bringing people the news," an official of the Freedom Forum explained to the Associated Press. A dedication ceremony was held in the spring of that year with First Lady Hillary Clinton, who invoked Lingan's name during her speech.

"When James Lingan was killed defending his newspaper's printing press from a mob in 1812, America was a young nation. We were still learning how to be a true democracy," she said, according to the *Baltimore Sun*.[129]

The journalism memorial was later moved and became part of the Newseum in Washington, D.C. The names of more than two thousand slain journalists are now included in the exhibit, but Lingan's name is no longer among them. His status as a journalist was reevaluated after the dedication, and his name was removed from the memorial. While there can be no doubting Lingan's courage in facing the mob, there is no evidence that he played an active role in the newspaper, other than supporting it financially. Noted Maryland historian Edward C. Papenfuse agreed that Lingan was not known for his journalism. "I frankly think his connection with the newspaper was remote, but his views were very much in line with those of Hanson and the newspaper," he told the *Sun* in 1996. "If you want to talk about free speech and taking strong stands in a newspaper, then the name Alexander Contee Hanson is the one."[130]

"Mobtown," Maryland

The Baltimore riots also bestowed a lasting legacy on the city itself. Long before Baltimore was known as Charm City or Monument City, it earned a less flattering moniker: Mobtown. One of the earliest known "Mob-Town" references came from a Federalist newspaper in New Jersey immediately after the jail massacre in August 1812. The name, in various iterations, was quickly adopted elsewhere, and by the fall, references could be found in newspapers in Massachusetts, New Hampshire and Pennsylvania.[131] The term was used in liberal doses as a synonym for the city, and some papers even substituted "Mob-Town" in the dateline for stories about Baltimore.

The *Federal Republican* referred to "mob-town" in a November 1812 issue, and even the anti-Federalist *Baltimore Patriot* acknowledged the nickname in several issues that fall. While we cannot offer definitive proof that the term "mob-town" did not appear in reference to Baltimore prior to the attack on Hanson's "Spartan Band"—a reference to "mob of the city" did appear after an 1807 riot—there can be little doubt the 1812 riots served as the foundation. The pejorative continued in regular use until the war with Great Britain concluded. After that, it appeared sparingly.

Gradually, the connection to the 1812 riots dissolved and perhaps some of the sting associated with it, but Baltimore's "Mobtown" nickname did not fade away—fairly or not. The 1812 riot was not the first riot in Baltimore and certainly not the last; nor was it the only major U.S. city to experience rioting during the nineteenth century. In fact, when riots beset the city of Philadelphia in the summer of 1840, one newspaper wryly suggested "the 'city of brotherly love' will now have to divide the honors consequent upon the name of 'mob-town' with Baltimore."

The connotation of the word *mob* shifted in the twentieth century, but Baltimore has stubbornly clung to—or in some cases warmly embraced—the mantle. Today, the city's "Mobtown" nickname is widely referenced in history texts and popular culture and firmly entrenched in the vernacular, as evidenced by the appearance of the "Mobtown" appellation in Facebook pages, dance halls, breweries, alternative newspapers and tourist attractions.

Contemporary historians often point to the "Mobtown" Massacre as a pivot point in the nation's history of social disorder: a transition from the civil, property-based rioting of the eighteenth century toward a more violent form of populist protest which endures today.[132]

Hanson, Massachusetts

On May 26, 1819, residents of Pembroke, Massachusetts, formally petitioned the state legislature to split off one section and form a new town. Situated in Plymouth County along the North River, Pembroke boasted a robust shipbuilding industry, but residents from the West Parish felt the distance was too far to travel for town meetings and argued that "peace, good order and economy would be greatly promoted"[133] if the local inhabitants could incorporate their own town.

The Massachusetts legislature was still under Federalist control at the time and included men like Josiah Quincy and Israel Thorndike, who knew Alexander Hanson personally and had even accompanied him on a fishing trip in nearby Hingham, Massachusetts, in 1813.[134] Hanson's former House colleague and Federalist ally Daniel Webster had also recently relocated to Massachusetts from New Hampshire.

The lead petitioner was Thomas Hobart, a Federalist attorney from Pembroke, who may also have met Hanson during his previous travels to New England. Hobart would later represent the new town in the legislature and was likely one of the driving forces in naming it in Hanson's honor. "An Act to Establish the Town of Hanson" was formally approved by the state legislature and signed into law by Governor John Brooks on February 22, 1820, ten months after Hanson's death.[135]

Years later, an aging Daniel Webster met a man who had visited the small town of Hanson, Massachusetts. Webster asked if he knew how the town got its name, according to one published report. When the man replied that he did not, Webster proceeded to tell the story about Alexander Hanson and explained how the townspeople "with a design to signatize their sympathy with law and order, and especially with the Federalism of the proscribed press, petitioned to have the town named Hanson in honor of the victims of the Baltimore mob."[136]

Today, Hanson, Massachusetts, serves as one of the few visible markers of the incandescent career of Alexander Hanson, a man who risked life and limb for the City of Baltimore, the state of American journalism and the nation's promise of a free press.

APPENDIX

THE EDITORIAL

Thou has done a deed, whereat valor will weep.

Without funds, without taxes, without an army, navy or adequate fortifications, with one hundred and fifty millions of our property in the hands of the declared enemy, without any of his in our power, and with a vast commerce afloat, our rulers have promulgated a war against the clear and decided sentiment of a vast majority of the nation. As the consequences will be so soon felt, there is no need of pointing them out to the few, who have not sagacity enough to apprehend them. Instead of employing our pen in this dreadful detail, we think it more apposite to delineate the course we are determined to pursue, as long as the war shall last. We mean to represent, in as a strong colors as we are capable, that it is unnecessary, inexpedient, and entered into from partial, personal, and as we believe, motives bearing upon their front marks of undisguised foreign influence, which cannot be mistaken.

We mean to use every constitutional argument and every legal means to render as odious and suspicious to the American people, as they deserve to be, the patrons and contrivers of this highly impolitic and destructive war, in the fullest persuasion, that we shall be supported and ultimately applauded by nine tenths of our countrymen, and that our silence would be treason to them.

We detest and abhor the endeavors of faction to create a civil contest through pretext of a foreign war, it has rashly and premeditetely [*sic*] commenced, and we shall be ready cheerfully to hazard every thing most dear, to frustrate any usurpation leading to the prostration of civil rights, and the establishment of a system of terror and proscription, announced in the government paper at Washington, as the inevitable consequence of the decisive measure now proclaimed. We shall cling to the rights of a freeman, both in act and opinion, till we sink with the liberty of our country, or sink alone. We shall hereafter as heretofore unravel every intrigue and imposture, which has beguiled or may be put forth to circumvent our fellow citizens into the toils of the great earthly enemy of the human race. We are avowedly hostile to the presidency of James Madison, and we never will breath under the dominion direct or derivative of Bonaparte, let it be acknowledged when it may. Let those who cannot openly adopt this confession, abandon us, and those who can, we shall cherish as friends and patriots, worthy of the name.

—*Federal Republican*, June 20, 1812

A NOTE ON SOURCES

This book would not be possible without the bounty of eyewitness accounts, depositions and related primary source materials, each offering a different bird's-eye view of the events before, during and after the attacks. Pieced together, they provide a remarkably detailed narrative of a series of events that occurred over two hundred years ago.

Chief among these is a report commissioned by the Maryland House of Delegates, which includes nearly eighty depositions, including ones from nearly all the key participants: *Grievances and Court of Justice of the House of Delegates of Maryland on the Subject of the Recent Mobs and Riots in the City of Baltimore*, published by Maryland House of Delegates, printed by Jonas Green, 1813. The executive report offers a fairly partisan summary of the episode, but the individual depositions offer firsthand accounts.

Hanson and his fellow Federalists published their own accounts a short time after the jail massacre: *An Exact and Authentic Narrative, of the Events which Took Place in Baltimore, on the 27th and 28th of July Last, Carefully Collected from Some of the Sufferers and Eye-Witnesses*, printed for the Purchasers, September 1, 1812. An additional narrative written by John Thompson was also included in the publication.

General "Light-Horse Harry" Lee published a separate account, though it was probably ghostwritten or dictated by him to someone else: *Correct Account of the Conduct of the Baltimore Mob, by Gen. Henry Lee, One of the Sufferers, Published by a Particular Friend, To which Is Prefixed as Introductory Detail of the Circumstance, Substantiated by Many Concurrent Evidences*, John Heiskell, printer, July 1814.

Other primary source accounts relied on include *Narrative of Otho Sprigg* and *Narrative of John E. Hall,* both published in the *Federal Republican* and later reprinted broadly. A compendium of primary source materials was published in *Interesting Papers Relative to the Recent Riots at Baltimore,* Philadelphia, 1812, which includes papers from the city council, the mayor and John Stricker.

An indispensable almanac of city residents containing addresses, occupations, street listings, businesses and census data is *Fry's Baltimore Directory,* compiled by William Fry and published by B.W. Sower & Co. I relied primarily on the 1810, 1812 and 1816 editions.

All quoted conversations, unless otherwise noted, are based on these primary sources. In cases where witnesses had conflicting recollections of the same conversations I have either presented each side or made an editorial judgment as to which account was more credible based on the available evidence. Whenever possible I have also corroborated key points of witness testimony with other accounts and known facts. The credibility of certain eyewitnesses was given added weight based on the level of detail and corroboration of their testimony.

In cases of spelling variations with names (Wolleslager is listed several different ways, for example) I have used the version listed in *Fry's Directory* or, in the case of rioters, the names as listed in the criminal court dockets for Baltimore County Court of Oyer and Terminer (July and September terms).

All weather-related data, unless noted, comes from *Father Abraham, Farmer's Almanac for the Year of Our Lord 1812, Warner & Hanna,* 1812 and entries in the *Journal of Captain Henry Thompson* as published by the Clifton House.

For a narrative often focused on newspapers, I naturally consulted many during my research. Fortunately, there are plenty of publications accessible from this period and many in electronic format, though some are subscription- or fee-based. The *Federal Republican, Federal Gazette, Hagers-town Gazette* and *Easton Star* are all available at genealogybank.com. The *Maryland Gazette* can be searched at newspapers.com and on the Maryland State Archives website. The *Baltimore American and Commercial Daily Advertiser* is available at Google news archive. I accessed issues of the *National Intelligencer* through the Boston Public Library's nineteenth-century newspaper database. The BPL also provides access to the British Library Newspapers database, including the *Times of London.* The *Niles' Weekly Register* is accessible at nilesregister.com. Limited issues of the *Baltimore Whig* and *Maryland Republican* are available online at the Maryland State Archives. The Historical Society of Frederick County assisted me with tracking down clips from the *Frederick-Town Herald.* The Massachusetts State Library and the Maryland Historical Society also have hardbound newspapers in their special collections. This by no means an exhaustive list but represents the publications I most frequently reviewed. Specific reference notes are cited in the text.

A bibliography is also listed at the end of the book. Early on, I found several previously published works particularly helpful and would like to thank authors Richard Chew, Paul Gilje and Donald Hickey for their research efforts. The endnotes offer an abridged version of sources used in this narrative, primarily in order to give credit to other authors, secondary sources and compiled collections of primary sources. Due to space restrictions, I have not included reference notes for every deposition from the primary source accounts noted above. More information is available at www.mobtownmassacre.com.

NOTES

Chapter 1

1. *Federal Republican* and role of the Federalist press, see Pasley, *Tyranny of Printers*, 229–57.
2. The Democratic-Republicans, often referred to simply as Republicans, were an offshoot of the Anti-Federalist movement, popularized by Thomas Jefferson. This Republican Party bears no direct relation to our modern-day Republican Party, which originated just before the Civil War. In fact, it would be more accurate to say that the Democratic-Republican Party grew into our modern-day Democratic Party. So these "Republicans" are actually closer to the party we now call "Democrats." It's not quite that simple of course—history rarely moves in such straight lines— but for the purposes of this narrative, we use the term "Republican" to refer to the Democratic-Republican Party since that was the customary usage of the time.
3. Rise and fall of Federalists party in Maryland generally, see Renzulli, *Maryland*, especially 228–53.
4. Hammond, *Colonial Mansions*, 175.
5. Ibid, 180.
6. Ibid, 181.
7. Cobbett, *Bloody Buoy*, 9.
8. Series of insults precipitating the duel is published in *Federal Republican*, May 5, 1809, 2. See also *Boston Repertory*, January 19, 1810, 2; *New-Hampshire Gazette*, January 23, 1810, 3; *Hampshire (MA) Federalist*, January 25, 1810, 3; *Federal Gazette* (Baltimore), January 12, 1810, 2; and *Hagers-town Gazette*, January 16, 1810, 3.
9. Hanson, *Old Kent*, 129.
10. See also Calderhead, "Strange Career," 373–86.

11. Hanson, *Trial of Alexander Contee Hanson*, 12–47.
12. *Frederick-Town Herald*, July 11, 1812, 2.
13. Visualizing Early Baltimore, "German Reformed Church," http://bearings. earlybaltimore.org.

Chapter 2

14. Merritt, "Baltimore's Original Marketplace."

Chapter 3

15. Hanson to George Carter, 1806, MdHS.
16. Hammond, *Colonial Mansions*, 74.
17. Ibid.
18. *Federal Gazette*, June 24, 1812, 3.
19. Steiner, *Life and Correspondence*, 580.
20. *Federal Gazette*, June 24, 1812, 3.
21. See "Legacy of Slavery in Maryland," MSA.
22. *Niles Weekly Register*, July 11, 1812, 305–8.
23. *American and Commercial Daily Advertiser*, July 8, 1812, 2.

Chapter 4

24. Pickering and Upham, *Life of Timothy Pickering* 212–13.
25. Pierce, "Memoirs," 378.
26. The letter was unsigned but is likely from Lee based on several factors: The Baltimore City Council in a later report identified Lee as the author. The letter was posted from Alexandria, and the contents track with his own military experience, including a reference to riding his horse. In his deposition, Hanson's friend John Howard Payne also described a paper written by Lee with details on the defensive measures for the house similar to the unsigned letter.

Chapter 5

27. "Just Received," *Federal Republican*, July 2, 1812, 4.
28. Steffen, *Mechanics of Baltimore*, 274–76.
29. Edward Papenfuse, "Recreating Lost Neighborhoods: The House on Ann Street, Fells Point, Baltimore City, Maryland," Thomas Poppleton's Baltimore, August 31, 2015, http://www.thomaspoppletonsbaltimore.net/2015/08/recreating-lost-neighborhoods-house-on.html.

30. *Federal Republican*, September 19, 1810, 3.
31. *Federal Gazette*, July 27, 1812, 4.

Chapter 6

32. "From the *Federal Republican*," *Norfolk Gazette*, September 14, 1812, 1.
33. Ibid.
34. Vile, *Wisest Council in the World*, quoting William Leigh Pierce poem, 33–34, 128–31.
35. Ibid.
36. Ibid.
37. Gilje, "'Le Menu Peuple,'" 53–64.
38. "From the Testimony of Henry Gaither, Esq.," *Federal Republican*, November 18, 1812, 2.

Chapter 7

39. Mayo, "Joshua Barney," 359–62.

Chapter 8

40. *Maryland Gazette*, August 27, 1812, 2 (from *Federal Republican*).
41. Varle, *Complete View of Baltimore*, 37–38; *Baltimore Price-Current*, July 25, 1812, 1.

Chapter 9

42. "Tragic-Comedy," *Federal Republican*, August 31, 1812, 2 (from *Greensborough Gazette*).

Chapter 10

43. "From the Repertory: The Massacre in Baltimore," *Newburyport (MA) Herald*, August 7, 1812, 2; "From the *Baltimore Whig*: The Peace and Dignity of the City," *American Watchman* (DE), August 5, 1812, 3.
44. Hanson, *An Accurate Report*, 46.

Chapter 11

45. "Extract of a Letter from Baltimore," *Connecticut Courant*, August 4, 1812, 3.

Chapter 12

46. Dorsey, "Biographical Sketch," 8.
47. Ridgely, *Historical Graves*, 250–52.
48. For Lingan's plea with mob, see Dorsey, "Biographical Sketch," 19.
49. *Frederick-Town Herald*, August 8, 1812.
50. Additional details on Thompson's beating in William Lansdale letter to Virgil Maxcy, August 3, 1812, LoC.
51. Letter of James W. Williams to John W. Stump, July 28, 1812, MdHS.
52. Goodson and Hollie, *Through the Tax Assessor*, 56, 200. See also Gilje, "'Le Menu Peuple.'"
53. Letter of James P. Boyd to James McHenry, August 2, 1812, MdHS.

Chapter 13

54. Tulloch, "Marking the Grave," 273.
55. Lingan's name was originally first on the Freedom Forum Journalist Memorial. See Hernandez, 1996.
56. Boyd to McHenry, August 2, 1812.

Chapter 14

57. *Federal Republican*, August 7, 1812, p. 3.
58. *Baltimore American and Commercial Daily Advertiser*, July 31, 1812, 3.
59. Gifford, *History of Wars*, 917.
60. *Poulson's American Daily*, July 31, 1812, 3.
61. *Evening Post* (New York), August 27, 1812, 2.
62. *New York Public Advertiser*, August 1, 1812, p. 2.
63. *Federal Republican*, August 3, 1812, 1–2.
64. Letter of William Patterson to John Patterson, July 30, 1812, MdHS.
65. Early references include *Carlisle (PA) Gazette*, August 7, 1812, 2; *Trenton Federalist*, August 10, 1812, 3; *Connecticut Herald*, August 11, 1812, 2.

Chapter 15

66. Letter from Hanson to John Hall, August 22, 1812, MdHS.
67. Benham, *Recollections of Old Alexandria*, 34.
68. *Thompson Journal*, July 30, 1812.
69. *Boston Repertory*, August 18, 1812, 2.
70. James Madison letter to John Montgomery, August 13, 1812, Founders Online, National Archives.

71. Ibid.; August 4, 1812.
72. *Federal Republican*, August 31, 1812, 3.
73. *Virginia Patriot*, August 11, 1812, 2; *National Intelligencer*, August 4, 1812, 3; *Pittsburgh Weekly Gazette*, August 14, 1812, 2.
74. *Federal Republican*, August 14, 1812, 3; August 19, 1812, 2.
75. Letter from Walter Dorsey and Edward J. Coale to Harrison G. Otis, August 20, 1812, MHS.
76. For subscription efforts, see *Federal Republican*, August 19, 1812, 2; *American Daily Advertiser*, September 8, 1812, 2 (from *Spirit of Seventy-Six*); *Newport Mercury*, August 22, 1812, 3; *Charleston Courier*, August 26, 1812, 2.
77. Hickey, *War of 1812*, 374 (endnote 131).
78. *Federal Republican*, August 17, 1812, 3.
79. *Hagers-town Gazette*, August 18, 1812, 2.
80. *Washington Courier*, August 27, 1812, 2.
81. *Niles Weekly Register*, September 19, 1812.
82. Congressman Charles Turner. See *Public Advertiser* (New York), August 12, 1812, 3; *Boston Patriot*, August 1, 1812, 1.
83. "Court Circular," *Times* (London), September 11, 1812, 3; "Untitled," September 14, 1812, 3; "American Papers," September 11, 1812, 2; "American Papers," October 29, 1812; *Hereford Journal* (Hereford, England), September 16, 1812, 4.
84. *Federal Republican*, August 19, 1812, 1.
85. *Washington Courier*, September 3, 1812, 2; *Federal Republican*, August 19, 1812, 1–2; *American and Commercial Daily Advertiser*, August 18, 1812, 2; *National Intelligencer*, September 5, 1812, 2 (quoting *Maryland Republican*).
86. Letter from Hanson to Priscilla Hanson, Rockville ("Sunday"), MdHS.

Chapter 16

87. Custis, *Recollections and Private Memoirs*, 572 (from explanatory note by unidentified author made at time Custis's original speech was published in pamphlet form).
88. Biographical Catalogue of Phillips Academy Andover, 1778–1830.
89. *National Intelligencer*, September 1, 1812, 7.
90. Ibid.
91. Ibid.
92. Ibid.
93. Custis, *Recollections and Private Memoirs*, 576.
94. *Federal Republican*, September 2, 1812, 3.
95. *Franklin (MA) Herald*, September 8, 1812, 4 (Reprinted from the *Repertory*).
96. *Charleston City Gazette*, September 19, 1812, 3.
97. Toasts published in *Federal Republican*, September 4, 1812, 3.
98. Ibid.

99. Hanson's opponent was John Linthicum, a former Federalist. Linthicum may have run without a formal party designation, but he became the de facto Republican choice and appeared on the Republican ticket in parts of the district.
100. Letter from Robert Goodloe Harper to Hanson, August 26, 1812, MdHS.
101. *Boston Repertory*, October 2, 1812, 2.

Chapter 17

102. Letter from Hanson to Edward Coale, September 22, 1812, MdHS.
103. *Courier* (Washington, D.C.), August 13, 1812, 2; *Republican Star*, August 18, 1812, 2; *American Watchman* (DE), August 15, 1812 (quoting *Baltimore Whig*).
104. *Federal Republican*, September 9, 1812, 2.
105. For relevant election laws, see Laws of Maryland –1805, Archives of Maryland Online, volume 141, page 516–19.
106. In a fractious presidential election, Madison later edged out dissident Republican DeWitt Clinton of New York to win reelection. A coalition of northern Republicans and Federalists was not quite enough to knock off Madison, who carried every southern state plus Vermont and Pennsylvania. In Maryland, turnout was high and the race was particularly close, but Madison ended up winning a 6–5 edge in Electoral College votes.

Chapter 18

107. Description of the statehouse, *Columbian Magazine*, 81–82.
108. White, *Southern Literary Messenger*, 346.
109. Ibid.
110. Anne Arundel County Court dockets, September 1812, MSA. See also *American Watchman*, November 18, 1812, 1; *Newburyport Herald*, October 16, 1812, 3; "Hanson's Trial," *Salem Gazette*, October 20, 1812, 1.

Epilogue

111. *Allegany Freeman* (Cumberland, MD), July 27, 1816, 6.
112. *Massachusetts Spy*, April 20, 1814, 4 (From the *New York Examiner*).
113. Van Tyne, *Letters of Daniel Webster*, 38. Letter from Webster to Chas. March.
114. *Connecticut Gazette*, October 10, 1813, 3; *Brattleboro Reporter*, July 3, 1813, 3; *Boston Yankee*, January 1, 1813, 3.
115. Hanson letter to John E. Hall, August 1813, MdHS.
116. During debate on the status of peace negotiations in the British House of Commons, reference was made to Federalists such as Hanson, who, it was felt, had turned against Great Britain after the attack on Washington. Hanson's

comments about the national bank and the bleak state of the U.S. finances were broadly republished, as was his criticism of preliminary British peace terms earlier in the fall, which he called "insulting and dishonorable." Those comments were interpreted abroad as being supportive of the Madison administration (though Hanson himself may not have concurred in that judgment). Still, the fact that leading Anglophiles who were once supportive of the United Kingdom's position had now soured was seen as an ominous development that strengthened the hand of American diplomats and ultimately may have pushed Great Britain toward peace. See "Vigourous Prosecution of the War in America," *Hull Packet and Original Weekly Commercial, Literary and General Advertiser* (Hull, England), November 1, 1814; "Imperial Parliament," *Caledonian Mercury* (Edinburgh), November 12, 1814; *Leeds Mercury* (Leeds, England), November 26, 1814; Wednesday and Thursday's Posts, *Northampton Mercury*, November 26, 1814, 2; "American Papers," *Morning Post* (London), November 1814; "Postscript," *Trewman's Exeter Flying Post or Plymouth and Cornish Advertiser* (Exeter, England), February 2, 1815; *Hull Packet and Original Weekly Commercial, Literary and General Advertiser*, February 7, 1815; all from British Library Newspapers, Part I: 1800–1900; and *New England Palladium*, February 14, 1815, 1.

117. *Baltimore Gazette and Daily Advertiser*, February 20, 1830, 3.

118. Panel & Smith v. The Farmer's Bank, 1826, Report of Cases, General Court and Court of Appeals of Maryland, March term, 1823, 203.

119. Inventory of the Goods, Chattels and personal estate of A. C. Hanson, November 30, 1819, Anne Arundel County Register of Wills, Box 145, Folder 46, Maryland State Archives.

120. Priscilla Hanson to Nicholas Worthington Mortgage, 1839, MdHS; *American and Commercial Daily Advertiser*, March 13, 1822, 4; October 25, 1822, 4.

121. "Nature and Power of the Slave States," *Boston Daily Atlas*, August 2, 1856, 2.

122. For more on this topic, including efforts of Hanson mentor Robert G. Harper, see Crenson, *Baltimore*, 165–67.

123. Gen. H. Lee letter to R. King, November 19, 1813, as published in King, *Life and Correspondence*.

124. Brock, *Gen. Robert Edward Lee*, 120–30.

125. Jones, *Reminiscences*, 15–33.

126. Stricker, "General John Stricker," 218.

127. *Boston Post*, September 8, 1859, 4; and *Public Ledger* (PA), September 22, 1859, 1.

128. "Lingan's Body Moved," *Baltimore Sun*, November 6, 1908, 8.; "Georgetown 'Harlem' Gone," *Washington Evening Star*, January 4, 1936, B2.

129. Hiaasen, "When an Editorial," 1E.

130. Ibid.

131. For early iterations see, *Trenton Federalist*, August 3, 1812, 3; *Baltimore Patriot*, August 10, 1813, 3; *Rhode Island American*, October 6, 1815, 2.

132. Gilje, *Rioting in America*. This new, more violent and chaotic strain of rioting was precipitated by the American Revolution, Gilje argues, but its fruits were first on display in Baltimore. "Against the rising tide of egalitarianism the world of corporatism crumbled like a sand castle besieged by pounding waves."

133. Bill packet, Acts and Resolves of 1819, Massachusetts Archives.

134. *Boston Daily Advertiser*, September 14, 1813, 2.

135. Acts and Resolves of 1819, Chapter 147, General Court of Massachusetts, February 22, 1820.

136. "Anecdotes of Daniel Webster," *Commercial Advertiser* (New York), April 4, 1871, 1. (Relating story from earlier interview in *Boston Daily Advertiser*).

SELECTED BIBLIOGRAPHY

Adams, Henry. *Documents Related to New England Federalism*. Boston: Little, Brown & Company, 1905.

Beirne, Francis. *The War of 1812*. New York: E.P. Dutton, 1949.

Benham, Mary Louisa. *Recollections of Old Alexandria and Other Memories*. Starkville, MS: Elizabeth Jane Stark, 1978.

Bogen, David. S. "The Annapolis Poll Books of 1800 and 1804: African American Voting in the Early Republic." *Maryland Historical Magazine* 86, no. 1 (1991): 57–65.

Bohmer, David A. "The Maryland Electorate and the Concept of a Party System in the Early National Period." In *The History of American Electoral Behavior*, by Joel Silbey and Allan Bogue, 146–73. Princeton, NJ: Princeton University Press, 1978.

Boyd, T.H.S. *The History of Montgomery County*. Bowie, MD: Heritage Books, 2001. Originally published 1879.

Brigham, Clarence. "History and Bibliography of American Newspapers, 1690–1820." *American Antiquarian Society* 2 (1947).

Brock, Robert A. *Gen. Robert Edward Lee: Soldier, Citizen, and Christian Patriot*. N.p.: B.F. Johnson Publishing Company, 1898.

Bruchey, Stuart R., et al. *Money and Banking in Maryland: A Brief History of Commercial Banking in the Old Line State*. Baltimore: Maryland Historical Society, 1996.

Brugger, Robert J. *Maryland: A Middle Temperament*. Baltimore: Johns Hopkins University Press, 1988.

Calderhead, William. "A Strange Career in a Young Navy: Captain Charles Gordon." *Maryland Historical Magazine* 72, no. 1 (1977): 373–86.

Cassell, Frank A. "The Great Baltimore Riots of 1812." *Maryland Historical Magazine* 70, no. 3 (1975): 241–59.

Chew, Richard. 2009. "The Origins of Mob Town: Social Division and Racial Conflict in Baltimore Riots of 1812." *Maryland Historical Magazine* 104, no. 3. (2009): 272–301.

Cobbett, William. *The Bloody Buoy, Thrown Out as a Warning to the Political Pilots of America.* Philadelphia, 1796.

Cordell F., Dr. Eugene. *Medical Annals of Maryland, 1799–1899.* Baltimore: The Medical and Chirurgical Faculty of the State of Maryland, 1903.

Coyle, William. *The Mayors of Baltimore.* N.p.: Baltimore Municipal Journal, 1919.

Cranwell, John Phillips, and William Bowers Crane. "The Log of the Rossie." *Maryland Historical Society Magazine* 35, no. 3 (1940): 287–91.

Crenson, Matthew A. *Baltimore, A Political History.* Baltimore: Johns Hopkins University Press, 2017.

Curtis, George T. *Life of Daniel Webster.* Vol. 1. New York: Appleton, 1870.

Custis, George Washington Parke. *Recollections and Private Memoirs of Washington.* New York: Derby & Jackson, 1860.

Delbourgo, James. *A Most Amazing Scene of Wonders: Electricity and Enlightenment in Early Americ.* Cambridge, MA: Harvard University Press, 2006.

Dennie, Charles C. "T. Gale, The Man of Mystery." *New York State Medical Journal*, no. 2 (1954): 400–5.

"Description of the State House at Annapolis, the Capital of Maryland." *Columbian Magazine* (1789).

Dorsey, Ella Loraine. "A Biographical Sketch of James Maccubbin Lingan." *Records of the Columbia Historical Society* 13: (1910): 1–48.

Dunn, John K., Jr. "'Their Shoes Yet New': The Immigrant Image in the Baltimore Riots of 1812 and the Disagreement Over Nationality." Honors thesis, University of Richmond, 2004.

Elfenbein, Jessica, John R. Breihan and Thomas L. Hollowak. *From Mobtown to Charm City: New Perspective's on Baltimore's Past.* Baltimore: Maryland Historical Society, 2002.

Farquhar, Roger Brooke. *Old Houses and History of Montgomery County, Maryland.* Baltimore: Maryland Historical Society, 1952.

Fay, Theodore Sedgwick. 1833. "A Sketch of the Life of John Howard Payne." *Boston Evening Gazette*, 1833.

Fischer, David. *The Revolution of American Conservatism.* New York: Harper & Row, 1965.

Fisher, Josephine. "Francis James Jackson and Newspaper Propoganda in the United States, 1809–1810." *Maryland Historical Society Magazine* 30, no. 2 (1935): 93–113.

Fletcher, Carlton. "Harlem." Glover Park History. October 20, 2017. http://gloverparkhistory.com/appendix/harlem.

Gates, John P. "A Monetary Misunderstanding, Smith v. Gilmor and Baltimore's Place in Turn of the 19th Century Globalization." University of Maryland Francis King Carey School of Law, 2012. https://digitalcommons.law.umaryland.edu/cgi/viewcontent.cgi?article=1040&context=student_pubs

Gelles, Auni. n.d. "Stricker House." Battle of Baltimore. Accessed May 15, 2018. www.battleofbaltimore.org/items/show/335.

Gifford, C.H. 1817. *History of Wars Occasioned by the French Revolution, from the Commencement of Hostilities in 1792 to the End of 1816.* W. Lewis.

Gilje, Paul A. "'Le Menu Peuple' in America: Identifying the Mob in the Baltimore Riots of 1812." *Maryland Historical Magazine* 81, no. 1 (1986): 53–55.

———. *Rioting in America.* Bloomington: Indiana University Press, 1996.

Gilmore, Robert. "Diary of Robert Gilmore (Published posthumously)." *Maryland Historical Magazine* 17, no. 3 (1922): 231–68.

Goodson, Noreen E., and Donna Tyler Hollie. *Through the Tax Assessor's Eyes: Enslaved People, Free Blacks and Slaveholders in Early Nineteenth Century Baltimore.* Baltimore: Clearfield Company, 2017.

Griffith, Thomas W. *Annals of Baltimore.* N.p.: William Wooddy, 1833.

Grosvenor, Thomas. *A Sketch of the Life, Last Sickness, and Death of Mary Jane Grosvenor.* Baltimore: Coale and Maxwell, 1817.

Hallmen, Sierra. "Sharp Street Memorial United Methodist Church." Explore Baltimore Heritage. https://explore.baltimoreheritage.org/items/show/520.

Hammond, John Martin. *Colonial Mansions of Maryland and Delaware.* Philadelphia: J.B. Lippincott, 1914.

Hanson, Alexander C. *An Accurate Report of the Argument, on the Motion of Attachment Against Baptis Irvine, Editor of the Whig, for a Contempt Against the Court of Oyer and Terminer for Baltimore County.* Baltimore: P.K. Wagner, 1808.

———. *Trial of Alexander Contee Hanson, Esq. A Lieutenant in a Company of Militia, Attached to the Thirty Ninth Regiment, Upon a Charge Conceived to be Mutinous and Highly Reproachful to the President and Commander in Chief of the Militia of the United States.* Baltimore: J. Robinson, 1812.

Hanson, George. *Old Kent: The Eastern Shore of Maryland.* Baltimore: Clearfield Company, 1990. Originally published 1876.

Hayward, Mary Ellen, and Frank R. Shivers Jr. *The Architecture of Baltimore: An Illustrated History.* Baltimore: Johns Hopkins University Press, 2004.

Hernandez, Debra Gersh. "In Memory." *Editor & Publisher,* June 8, 1996.

Hiaasen, Rob. "When an Editorial Could Get You Killed." *Baltimore Sun,* May 24, 1996, 1E.

Hickey, Donald R. "Darker Side of Democracy: The Baltimore Riots of 1812." *Maryland Historian* 7, no. 2 (1976).

———. *The War of 1812: A Forgotten Conflict.* Urbana: University of Illinois Press, 2012.

Hume, Edgar Erskine. "Light-Horse Harry and His Fellow Members of the Cincinnati." *Omohundro Institute of Early American History and Culture* 15, no. 3 (1935): 271–81.

Irvin, Benjamin. "Tar, Feathers, and the Enemies of American Liberties, 1768–1776." *New England Quarterly* 76, no. 2 (2003).

Jackson, Richard P. *The Chronicles of Georgetown, D.C.* Westminster, MD: Heritage Books, 2011. First published 1878.

Janik, Erika L., and Matthew B. Jensen. "Every Man His Own Electric Physician: T. Gale and the History of Do-It-Yourself Neurology." *Journal of Neurological Research and Therapy* 1 (2016): 17–22. As published in *U.S. National Institutes of Health's PubMed* (2016).

Jones, Charles C. *Reminiscences of the Last Days, Death and Burial of General Henry Lee.* Albany, NY: Joel Munsell, 1870.

Keidel, George C. "Early Maryland Newspapers." *Maryland Historical Magazine* 30, no. 2 (1933).

Keyssar, Alexander. 2009. *The Right to Vote: The Contested History of Democracy in the United States.* New York: Basic Books, 2009.

King, Charles. *The Life and Correspondence of Rufus King.* New York: G.P. Putnam & Sons, 1895.

King, Quentin S. *Henry Clay and the War of 1812.* Jefferson, NC: McFarland and Company, 2014.

Latrobe, John H.B. Jr. n.d. "Baltimore Jail: 'Troubled Times' at the Baltimore Gaol." Battle of Baltimore. Accessed September 21, 2017. https://www.battleofbaltimore.org.

"Legacy of Slavery in Maryland." Maryland State Archives. Accessed April 2017. http://slavery.msa.maryland.gov.

Lewis, Jeffrey, Brandon DeVine, Lincoln Pitcher and Kenneth Martis. "Digital Boundary Definitions of United States Congressional Districts, 1789–2012." United States Congressional Districts Shapefiles. Accessed January 7, 2018. http://cdmaps.polisci.ucla.edu.

Lim, Elvin T. *The Lovers' Quarrel: The Two Foundings and American Political Development.* New York: Oxford University Press, 2013.

Lossing, Benson J. *The Pictorial Field-book of the War of 1812: Or, Illustrations, by Pen and Pencil, of the History, Biography, Scenery, Relics, and Traditions of the Last War for American Independence.* New York: Harper & Brothers, 1869.

Marine, William M. *British Invasion of Maryland: 1812–1815.* Baltimore: Society of the War of 1812, 1913.

Mason, Matthew. *Slavery and Politics in the Early American Republic.* Chapel Hill: University of North Carolina Press, 2008.

Mayo, Bernard. "Joshua Barney and the French Revolution." *Maryland Historical Society Magazine* 36, no. 4 (1941).

McCauley, Lois, ed. *Maryland Historical Prints.* Baltimore: Maryland Historical Society, 1975.

McCullough, David. *1776.* New York: Simon and Schuster, 2005.

McGrain, John W. "The Development and Decline of Dorseys Forge." *Maryland Historical Society Magazine,* 72, no. 3 (1977): 346–52.

McKendry, David Ian. "The Ghosts of the American Revolution: The HMS Jersey Prison Ship." 13th Floor. Accessed October 20, 2017. http://www.the13thfloor.tv/2016/01/29/the-ghosts-of-the-american-revolution-the-hms-jersey-prison-ship.

McWilliams, Jane Wilson. *Annapolis: City on the Severn*. Baltimore: Johns Hopkins University Press and Maryland Historical Trust Press, 2011.

Merritt, James M. "Baltimore's Original Marketplace." *Baltimore Sun*, December 1, 1993.

Mould, David, and Missy Loewe. *Remembering Georgetown: A History of the Lost Port City*. Charleston, SC: Arcadia Publishing, 2009.

Neimeyer, Charles. *War in the Chesapeake: The British Campaigns to Control the Bay, 1813–1814*. Annapolis, MD: Naval Institute Press, 2015.

New Nation Votes: American Election Returns 1787–1825. Tufts University Digital Collections Archive and American Antiquarian Society. Accessed January 18, 2018. https://elections.lib.tufts.edu.

Papenfuse Edward, et al. *A Biographical Dictionary of the Maryland Legislature 1635–1789*. Vol. 1. Baltimore: Johns Hopkins University Press, 1979.

Pasley, Jeffrey. *The Tyranny of Printers*. Charlottesville: University of Virginia Press, 2001.

Phillips, Christopher. *Freedom's Port: The African American Community of Baltimore, 1790–1860*. Urbana: University of Illinois Press, 1997.

Pickering, Octavius, and Charles W. Upham. *The Life of Timothy Pickering*. Vol. 4. Boston: Little, Brown and Company, 1873.

Pierce, Dr. John. "The Reverend Dr. John Pierce Memoirs." *Proceedings of the Massachusetts Historical Society* 19 (1905): 379.

Ramsburgh, Edith R., and A.Y. Casanova. "Distinguished Marylanders in St. Memim Collection." *Daughters of the American Revolution Magazine* 56, no. 1 (1922): 600–606.

Renzulli, L. Marx Jr., *Maryland: The Federalist Years*. Madison, NJ: Fairleigh Dickinson University Press, 1972.

Rice, Jim. "This Province, So Meanly and Thinly Inhabited: Punishing Maryland's Criminals." *Journal of the Early Republic* 19, no. 1 (1999): 15–42.

Rice, Laura. *Maryland History in Prints 1743–1900*. Baltimore: Maryland Historical Society, 2002.

Ridgely, Helen. *Historical Graves of Maryland and the District of Columbia*. New York: Grafton Press, 1908.

Royster, Charles. *Light Horse Harry Lee and the Legacy of the American Revolution*. New York: Alfred Knopf, 1981.

Scharf, J. Thomas. *The Chronicles of Baltimore*. Baltimore: Turnbull Brothers, 1874.

Schauinger, Joseph. "Alexander Contee Hanson, Federalist Partisan." *Maryland Historical Magazine* 34, no. 4 (1922): 354–64.

Semmes, John E. *John H.B. Latrobe and His Times 1803–1891*. Baltimore: Norman Remington Co., 1917.

Shugg, Wallace. *A Monument to Good Intentions*. Baltimore: Maryland Historical Society, 2000.

Spaulding, Myra. *Dueling in the District of Columbia*. Historical Society of Washington, D.C., 1928.

Steffen, Charles G. *The Mechanics of Baltimore*. Urbana: University of Illinois Press, 1984.

Steiner, Bernard C. *The Life and Correspondence of James McHenry*. Cleveland, OH: Burrows Brothers Company, 1912.

Steuart, Rieman. *A History of the Maryland Line in the Revolutionary War*. Washington, D.C.: Society of the Cincinnati of Maryland, 1969.

Stockbridge, Henry Sr. "Baltimore in 1846." *Maryland Historical Magazine* 6, no. 1 (1911): 20–34.

Stone, Kristin. "Under a Cloak of Nationalism: Wrangling Public Opinion during the War of 1812." *Maryland Historical Magazine* 110, no. 3 (2015): 313–39.

Stricker, John Jr. "General John Stricker." *Maryland Historical Magazine* 9, no. 3 (1914): 209–18.

Thompson, Henry. "Journal of Henry Thompson of Clifton and Captain of the First Baltimore Horse Artillery." Unpublished manuscript. Baltimore: Friends of Clifton Mansion, 1812.

Tulloch, B.C. "Marking the Grave of a Hero." *American Monthly Magazine* (1903).

Updyke, Frank A. *The Diplomacy of the War of 1812*. Baltimore: Johns Hopkins University Press, 1915.

Van Tyne, C.H. *The Letters of Daniel Webster, from Documents Owned Principally by the New Hampshire Historical Dociety*. New York: McClure, Phillips & Company, 1902.

Varle, Charles. *A Complete View of Baltimore with a Statistical Sketch*. Baltimore: Samuel Young, 1833.

Vile, John R. *The Wisest Council in the World: Restoring the Character Sketches by William Pierce of Georgia of the Delegates to the Constitutional Convention of 1787*. Athens: University of Georgia Press, 2015.

Visualizing Early Baltimore: City of Baltimore circa 1815. University of Maryland, Accessed May 2017. http://bearings.earlybaltimore.org.

Vogel, Steve. *Through the Perilous Fight: Six Weeks That Saved the Nation*. New York: Random House, 2013.

White, T. Stephen. *The Price of Freedom: Slavery and Manumission in Baltimore and Early National Maryland*. Lexington: University Press of Kentucky, 2015.

White, T.W. "Jeremiah T. Chase." *Southern Literary Messenger* 4, no. 6 (1838).

Winchester, Paul, and Frank Webb. 1905. "Newspapers and Newspaper Men of Maryland Past & Present." Baltimore: Journalists Club of Baltimore (F.L. Sibley & Sons), 1905.

Winter, Aaron McLean. 2009. "The Laughing Doves of 1812 and the Satiric Endowment of Antiwar Rhetoric in the United States." *PMLA* 124, no. 5 (2009): 1562–81.

Wright, F. Edward, ed. *Maryland Militia in the War of 1812*. Vol. 2. Lewes, DE: Colonial Roots, 2006.

INDEX

ABOUT THE AUTHOR

J osh S. Cutler is an attorney and state legislator, representing the Sixth Plymouth District of Massachusetts, which includes the town of Hanson. Like Alexander Hanson, he is also a former newspaper editor, though he's never been attacked by a mob! Cutler is a graduate of Skidmore College (BA), Suffolk Law (JD) and the University of Massachusetts at Dartmouth (MPP in Environmental Policy). He is also the author of "When the Press Really Was Under Attack: Alexander Hanson and the 1812 'Mobtown' Massacre" published by the *New England Journal of History* (Spring 2018). When he's not hot on the trail of nineteenth-century Federalist agitators, Cutler enjoys photography, traveling, hiking and spending time with his children, Charlie and Delilah.

All royalties from the sale of *Mobtown Massacre: Alexander Hanson and the Baltimore Newspaper War of 1812* will be donated to the Baltimore City Historical Society and the Hanson Historical Society.